# The **Big Book** of WITHDRAWN
# Bird Houses
# & Bird Feeders

# The **Big Book** of Bird Houses & Bird Feeders

How to Build Unique Bird Houses, Bird Feeders and Bird Baths from the Purely Practical to the Simply Outrageous

THOM BOSWELL,
BRUCE WOODS &
DAVID SCHOONMAKER

Sterling Publishing Co., Inc.
New York

Material in this book previously appeared in
The Bird Feeder Book © 1993 by Altamont Press
The Bird House Book © 1991 by Altamont Press

2   4   6   8   10   9   7   5   3   1

Published by Sterling Publishing Co., Inc.
387 Park Avenue South, New York, NY 10016
© 2004 by Sterling Publishing Co., Inc.

Distributed in Canada by Sterling Publishing
c/o Canadian Manda Group, One Atlantic Avenue, Suite 105
Toronto, Ontario, Canada M6K 3E7
Distributed in Great Britain by Chrysalis Books
64 Brewery Road, London N7 9NT, England
Distributed in Australia by Capricorn Link (Australia) Pty. Ltd.
P.O. Box 704, Windsor, NSW 2756, Australia

Printed in China

Sterling ISBN 1-4027-1373-8

# CONTENTS

# Introduction

If you've never built a bird feeder or house, a wonderful adventure awaits you. Not only are they fun to build and a great way to ornament your yard, you'll get to watch them being used by a fascinating variety of birds you may barely have known existed. If you've already tried your hand at this craft or installed storebought structures, this book will inspire you to stretch the limits of your imagination and skills, and will even help you design your own.

There's something in this book for everyone, from children to experienced woodworkers. While most of the projects are constructed of wood, you'll be introduced to several other accessible materials and techniques as well. And while each project is explained with specific instructions, you are encouraged to adapt and experiment with these designs to suit yourself. Essentially, this book contains the "blueprints" for forty fascinating bird structures, yet it also serves as a manual that will equip you to exercise your own creativity.

Providing shelter, food and water for birds is a human pastime that extends far back into history. In medieval Europe, this was actually a way of harvesting birds to supplement their own meager diets. Native Americans used to hang gourd houses for purple martins who would chase vultures away from their meat drying racks. Gardeners like to attract certain birds to help control insect populations that can destroy vegetation. Martins, robins, wrens, thrushes, warblers, swallows and bats are all excellent exterminators and reduce the need for chemical pesticides.

Of course, there are other reasons for nurturing our feathered friends that are less self-serving. As human civilization continues to encroach on wilderness, we are obliged to provide habitat for species that have been denied their natural feeding and nesting sites. We can also lure species back into refurbished areas they'd been forced to abandon.

Birding, or bird watching, is growing in popularity, especially in the U.S. and the British Isles. People have a natural appreciation and concern for birds. Sitings are compiled in "life lists," and copious field notes document behavior. The best bird structure designs are those which utilize this sort of information.

Constructing habitat for birds need not be such an exacting science, however. Many a bird will find comfort in even the most amateur of attempts at feeder or house building. Neither may it matter to you precisely which species comes to feed or takes up residence in your generically constructed house. The antics of sparrows can be just as much fun to watch as the flitting colors of a finch.

There are others yet who see these structures as an art form. A "house" need not be a "home," and a feeder or bath can be elaborately sculpted for the absolute delight of humans, yet be nothing more than a curious perch for birds. People who dabble with doll houses or miniatures will love the possibilities of art for the birds. In fact, some of the more detailed and exquisite structures in this book would be better appreciated indoors than out.

As you can see in our gallery (pages 30-57) most examples of this art form are houses instead of feeders. Curiously, feeders are more popular than houses. Maybe it's time to start elevating feeders to the level of art, too, as this book begins to do. Whether for function or fancy, you can take part in this enjoyable creative process.

*"Eats Diner"* by Randy Sewell

# Design Considerations

## Types of Feeders

There are several basic types of feeders, each designed to dispense certain feeds and to accommodate the feeding habits of different birds. These are some of the features to consider when choosing a design for your feeder:

1. Maximize the load capacity of the feed container for less frequent refilling.

2. Make the feed container easy to open to facilitate refilling.

3. If there's a roof, it should effectively protect the seed from rain and snow.

4. Provide drainage outlets in the feed tray to prevent stagnant pooling of water.

5. Incorporate a spill tray with a lip or plexiglass wall so birds can see the feed.

6. Provide adequate space for birds to perch and eat.

7. Make it as easy as possible to take apart and clean.

Here are the most common types of feeders, each of which has many design possibilities:

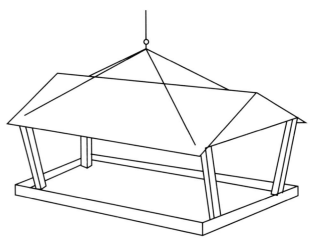

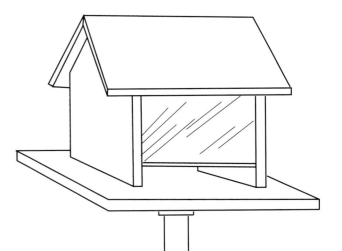

**Ground or Open Tray** feeders are among the simplest of approaches to dispensing feed. You can attract a wide variety of birds, such as cardinals, jays, sparrows, doves and chickadees, by scattering cracked corn or mixed seed directly on the ground. Choose a clearing of cropped lawn, dirt or patio and sprinkle seed over an eight-foot circle. However, constructing a simple post-mounted tray has several advantages for you and the birds. If you add a lip to contain the seed, allow for drainage with gaps in the lip or holes in the tray. This type of feeder should be mounted about five feet above ground and is very easy to refill and clean.

**Roofed Tray** feeders protect feed from the elements. The roof should be larger than the tray, and can be supported by a center post, peripheral posts, or even suspended from above. This open-air structure lends itself to all sorts of pavilion and gazebo-type designs, and is a highly functional feeder.

**Hopper** feeders are quite prevalent because they incorporate so many desirable features. The major feature, in addition to tray and roof, is a feed container that gradually dispenses feed through some sort of openings, usually onto the tray. The roof may cover both hopper and feeding tray, or the hopper only. Some of the walls might be transparent.

**Tube** feeders are very popular, usually clear plastic to display the feed, and mounted on post or by hanging. They have multiple holes with perches around the cylinder for feeding stations, and often feature a bottom dish and protective roof dome. They are easily refilled, and may incorporate metal-reinforced holes and perches that squirrels cannot chew.

**Suet** feeders require different structures because of the globular consistency of the suet. A plastic-coated wire cage works well. One-inch diameter holes can be drilled in a hanging log, post or stump and filled with suet. An inverted hanging cup (coconut half, yogurt canister or bell) packed with suet will attract chickadees. These can be hung from a tree or the eaves of a house, or fastened to a tree trunk. They are especially visited in winter, and attract woodpeckers, nuthatches and mocking-birds, among others.

**Mesh Bag** feeders are very simple and can also be attached to other sorts of feeders. Just fill a plastic mesh bag (such as onions are sold in) with nuts or thistle seed, and hang it to attract finches, buntings and chickadees.

Many birds prefer to light on a good vantage point and survey the situation before swooping down to feed or bathe. If there are no trees or tall structures in the vicinity of your feeder or bath, you can build a simple perch or two. Nail a short cross-piece on top of an 8'–12' pole and plant it nearby.

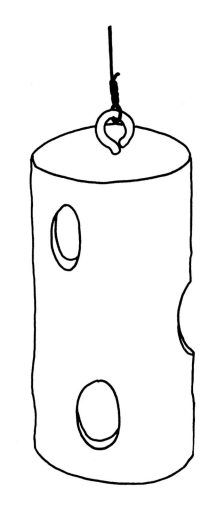

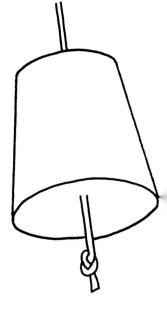

# Types of Baths

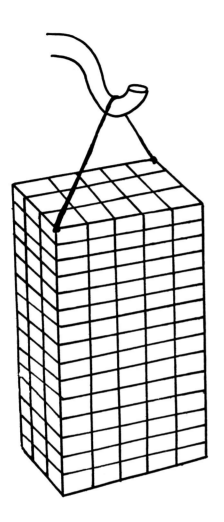

All birds need water for drinking and bathing. Most birds scoop water into their bills and tilt their heads back to drink. Others, like doves, can actually sip. Bathing behavior includes some fascinating variations as well. Many birds stand in shallow water and funnel it into and out of their feathers using complex body movements. Some take a quick dive and fly out while others fully submerge for a bit. Birds will also bathe in rain or dew drops.

Your bath will be visited more frequently if you place it near a feeder. It can be on or above the ground. When making or purchasing a bath, keep in mind that it should be shallow with gradual slopes so that birds can wade in to a depth of no more than three inches of water. The surface should not be slippery. Avoid ceramics if the water will freeze in winter because they will crack. Concrete works well and can be molded, especially when reinforced, into any shape on or above ground. You may want to incorporate one or more small pools in your landscaping. Even an inverted trash can lid will serve the purpose.

The sound of running water is especially attractive to birds. This can be achieved in several ways. Drip hoses and mist fountains are commercially available for this purpose. You can also erect a reservoir, such as a bucket, over your bath that has a tiny drip hole. This will, of course, require refilling.

Birds also need water during cold dry spells in winter. To keep the water in your bath from freezing, you can purchase an inexpensive electric water heater that is designed for bird baths. Scrub out your bath periodically with fresh water and a brush.

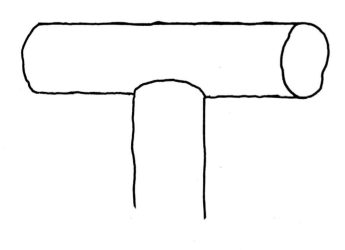

# Types of Houses

When you consider how many birds take up residence in unlikely nooks and crannies, it would seem that they're not very particular about housing requirements. However, each species has its own specific needs regarding the dimensions of its living chamber, the size and position of entry hole, siting, etc. Also, it is surprisingly difficult to lure most bird species into man-made houses. Even the colors you paint your house will affect its habitability. Birds generally prefer natural muted hues, although purple martins are attracted to white.

The chart on the following pages lists guidelines for many common species, but bear in mind that bird-house design is not an exact science. You can learn a lot simply by observing the behavior and nesting habits of whatever birds are common in your region. Build the chamber or platform according to the size of the bird you wish to attract. Place it in a site comparable to its preferred habitat. If it builds nests in the open, it should prefer a platform type of house. If it nests in a tree hole or other crevice, you will need to construct a chamber. Note which species are common to your area and alter your designs to accommodate them.

It must also be noted, however, that a number of designs are intended more for human amusement and decoration than bird utilization. Bird structures have become an art form in their own right, and are displayed in parlors and galleries as well as back-yards and public parks. And who knows, maybe some odd bird will share your aesthetic and adapt its needs to your sense of whimsy.

12

Most bird houses can be divided roughly into four categories, each of which offers numerous design possibilities:

**Platform** houses are preferred by certain claustrophobic species such as robins. They can be mounted on a pole, cradled in a tree or hung on a wall. They occasionally have one or two walls which facilitate wall mounting or act as a windbreak.

**Open Box** houses can vary significantly, depending on size, siting, and which part is left open. Barn owls can do without a roof when the box is inside a much larger structure. Kestrels and flycatchers like having one wall open. Bats need open floors for bottom entry. Mounting and siting will vary greatly depending on the species.

**Enclosed** houses are the most common since they appeal to the widest variety of birds. The floors of these chambers are recessed in the sense that the entry hole is above floor level. There is tremendous variance in all other design elements, mounting and siting.

**Multi-Compartment** houses have very limited appeal, being suited only to communal dwellers like purple martins and bats. Purple martin houses are mounted high on poles or rooftops. Bat houses are mounted high in trees or on poles. The number of compartments can vary greatly.

# Some House-Nesting Birds

| Species | Approximate Dimensions | Hole Dimensions |
|---|---|---|
| **Bluebird** (Eastern, Western, and Mountain)[1]<br>Sialia spp. | Floor: 5" x 5"<br>Interior height: 8" to 10" | Height above floor (centered): 6"<br>(5" for Warbler)<br>Diameter: 1-1/2" |
| **Chickadee** (Black-capped, Boreal, and Carolina)[2]<br>Parus spp. | Floor: 4" x 4"<br>Interior height: 8" to 10" | Height above floor (centered): 6"<br>Diameter: 1-1/4" |
| **Finch** (House and Purple)<br>Carpodacus spp. | Floor: 6" x 6"<br>Interior height: 6" | Height above floor (centered): 3"–4"<br>Diameter: 2" |
| **Flicker**<br>Colaptes auratus | Floor: 7" x 7"<br>Interior height: 16"+ | Height above floor (centered): 12"+<br>Diameter: 2-3/4" |
| **Flycatcher** (Many varieties)<br>Tyrannus spp., Myiarchus spp. | Floor: 6" x 6"<br>Interior height: 14" | Height above floor (centered): 6"+<br>Diameter: 2" |
| **Jackdaw** (Corvus moredula) | Floor: 8" x 8"<br>Interior height: 12" | Height above floor (centered): 6"<br>Diameter: 6" |
| **Owl** (Barn)<br>Tyto alba | Floor: 10" x 18"<br>Interior height: 18" | Height above floor (centered): 4"<br>Diameter: 6" |
| **Owl** (Saw-whet, Screech and Little)<br>Aegolius acadicus, Otus asio and Athene noctua | Floor: 10" x 10"<br>Interior height: 15" | Height above floor (centered): 10"+<br>Diameter: 3" |
| **Pigeon** (Street)<br>Columba livia | Floor: 8" x 8"<br>Interior height: 8" | Height above floor (centered): 4"<br>Diameter: 4" |
| **Purple Martin**<br>(Progne subus) | Floor: 6" x 6"<br>Interior height: 6"<br>(each compartment) | Height above floor (centered): 1-3/4"<br>Diameter: 2-1/2" |
| **Robin** (American and English)[3]<br>Tardus migratorius and Erithacus rubecula | Floor: 6" x 6"<br>Interior height: 8"<br>(open roofed platform) | No hole, open-sided roofed box |
| **Sparrows** (House and many others)<br>Passer domesticus, members of Family Fringillidae | Floor: 10" x 10"<br>Interior height: 15"+ | Height above floor (centered): 6"<br>Diameter: 1-1/2" |
| **Wood Duck** [4]<br>Aix sponsa | Floor: 6" x 6"<br>Interior height: 14"+ | Height above floor (centered): 12"–16"<br>(9"–12" for Kestrel)<br>Diameter: 3" x 4" (oval)<br>Add interior ramp covered<br>with chicken wire |
| **Woodpecker** (Hairy, Red-bellied, Red-cockaded, Red-headed, and Yellow-bellied Sapsucker)<br>Picoides villosus, Melanerpes carolinus,<br>Picoides borealis, Melanerpes erythrocephalus,<br>and Sphyrapicus varius | Floor: 8" x 8"<br>Interior height: 24" | Height above floor (centered): 9"–12"<br>Diameter: 1-1/2" (Hairy, Red-bellied,<br>Red-cockaded, Sapsucker)<br>2" (Red-headed) |
| **Woodpecker** (Pileated)<br>Dryocopus pileatus | Floor: 4" x 4"<br>Interior height: 14" | Height above floor (centered): 10"<br>Diameter: 4" |
| **Wrens** (House, Bewick's, Carolina, and others)<br>Family Troglodytidae | Floor: 4" x 4"<br>Interior height: 8" | Height above floor (centered): 4"<br>Diameter: 1-1/4" (House), 1-1/2"<br>(Bewick's, Carolina, and others) |

[1] House will also serve: Tree Swallow (Iridoprocne bicolor), Warblers (Parula spp.), Spotted Flycatcher (Muscicapa striata)

[2] House will also serve: Brown Creeper (Certhia familiaris), Downy Woodpecker (Picoides pubescens), Nuthatches (Sitta spp.), Tufted Titmouse (Parus bicolor)

| Height Above Ground | Siting Tips |
|---|---|
| 5'–10' | On fence posts, stumps, utility poles, tree trunks, etc. Place around open fields or any grassy expanse (park, cemetary, golf course). Predator collar suggested. |
| 6'–15' | Locate near large trees, Line with non-aromatic wood shavings. |
| 8'–12' | Both birds primarily Western though sometimes found in East. Purple Finch prefers wooded site. |
| 6'–20' | Site on tree trunk, line bottom with 3"+ of non-aromatic sawdust. |
| 8'–20' | Prefers wooded site, natural-appearing house. |
| 10'+ | Away from human noise. |
| 12'–20' | Locate near open fields/meadows to provide hunting range. |
| 10'–30' | Near water if at all possible. Prefers open yard with few or no trees nearby. |
| 10'+ | Prefers a perch. |
| Above reach of cats | Prefers open area near well-maintained lawns for feeding. |
| 12' | Habitats vary widely. |
| 10'–20' | Locate on trees or buildings. |
| 12'–20' | Wood Duck: Locate near (or above) water, line with 3"+ non-aromatic sawdust, predator collar suggested. Kestrel: Site on edge of field or meadow to provide hunting range. |
| 12'–20' | Site on tree trunk, much prefers natural-looking house (bark lined, for example) |
| 6'–10' | Locate among large trees. Natural-looking house essential. |
| 6'–10' | Site on edge of woods, in fencerows, etc. |

[3] House (nesting platform) will also serve: Barn Swallow (Riparia riparia), Phoebes, Eastern and Say's (Sayornis spp.), Various Thrushes (Cartharus spp.), Song Sparrow (Melospiza melodia), Pied Wagtail (Motacilla alba)

[4] House will also serve: American Kestrel (Falco sparvarius), European Kestrel (Falco tinnunculus)

Your birdhouse will be occupied only a few months each year by migrating birds. Wait until spring to clean out the house to allow winter birds like chickadees and bluebirds to use the old nesting material. To enable cleaning, design one panel of your house to be hinged or removable. It could be the roof, floor, or any wall. After you have removed all the old nesting material, pour boiling water over the interior to kill any remaining parasites.

Most houses will benefit from ventilation and drainage. Small holes or slots can be cut around the roof eaves for vents. Drill 1/8" drain holes in the corners of the floor.

The entry hole is a crucial part of any house. If it's too large it will invite intruders. If it's too small or high it will hinder access. If it's too low it will admit harsh weather. To discourage predators, you can cut a doughnut-shaped piece of 1 x stock that conforms to your entry hole and attach it inside to extend the portal. Roughen this tunnel with a rasp to accommodate the grip of bird claws.

Varying the shape and material of the roof is a great way to add interest to your birdhouse or feeder. Some basic shapes to consider are shed, gabled, hip, mansard, gambrel, pyramidal, conical and domed. Materials can include solid wood, plywood, bark-faced slab, cedar shakes or doll house shingles, tar paper, fiberglass shingles, sheet metal, copper, bamboo and thatch. Generally, the steeper the roof, the less it is prone to leaking. Just make sure the ridge is caulked to seal it. A flat roof requires the protection of an impervious sealant, as do the edges of plywood where the glue seams of lamination will separate.

# Unwanted Guests

It's a jungle out there—and that's just the way it should be. As much as we might prefer well-mannered songbirds with exquisitely colorful plumage, nature's panorama reminds us that the weak must fall prey to the strong, and there is beauty in all creation. Swallows and swifts may clog our chimneys with their nests, but they also devour tons of bothersome mosquitos.

Ultimately, human intervention plays its part in this grand scheme. We are free to nurture and protect our feathered friends with food and shelter. And to do this effectively, we must learn how to counteract the competition and predation that would undo our efforts. Here, then, are profiles of the bird world's ten most unwanted list.

## Sparrows

Most varieties of sparrow will nest almost anywhere, including your attic if they find entry. If you've built your house for a less common species, you'll want to discourage them from setting up housekeeping. Since they tend to nest earlier in the season than most birds, you can probably clean out their nests before your intended guests arrive. Also, they are much less likely to nest if you leave off the porch under your entry hole.

Sparrows will also be frequent customers at your feeder. This is really not a problem, unless your feed is limited or you're hoping to attract different birds. If you don't want sparrows, stock your feeder with red proso millet, Niger thistle and peanuts.

## Starlings

There's no easy way to keep starlings from nesting in your birdhouse. Like the sparrow, the undesirability of the starling has mostly to do with its commonality. Your best bet is to build your birdhouse strictly to the specifications outlined in the chart on pages 14 and 15.

There's little competition at most feeders, however, since starlings are primarily suet-eaters. Keep this in mind when you stock suet for other birds.

### Cats

Be aware of feline territories when you install a birdhouse or feeder. Let's face it, cats love birds, but assuming they're domesticated they will playfully torture a bird rather than consuming an honest meal. Mount your house, bath or feeder above leaping range. Install a predator barrier on tree or pole. Put a bell on your cat's collar. Eliminate low foliage where cats can hide as they wait to pounce, and keep grass mowed around feeders.

### Dogs

Dogs aren't nearly as dangerous as cats, but can still pose a threat if you don't take precautions. You could perhaps verbally discourage your dog, or your neighbor's dog, but you'll most likely have success by fencing the bird zone away from dog territories. A dog's very presence can keep more timid birds from visiting your beautifully prepared sites.

### Raccoons, Skunks and Oppossum

If you live in a rural or semi-rural environment, these predators may be looking for a quick meal. Follow the same precautions necessitated by cats, plus a tight mesh fence. You may also elect to control the threat by setting out traps. We would encourage the use of live traps, such as the Hav-a-hart brand. If you believe you must kill these animals, check with your local fish and game authorities and know what you're doing.

### Hawks and Shrikes

An attack by these large birds on smaller birds would be natural and horribly fascinating, but

quite unlikely. If you'd like to create a defense for your smaller birds, provide them with lots of nearby places to seek shelter should they be assaulted. The most likely marauders are the sharp-shinned hawks in the eastern U.S. and Cooper's hawks in the western U.S. Do keep in mind that hawks are protected by laws, as well as nature's plan.

## Squirrels

These cute little creatures are probably a bird's most prevalent pest. The squirrels' legendary attraction to bird feeders can become a consuming preoccupation for us as human hosts, but needs to be taken in perspective. You may as well expect a certain level of squirrel piracy as inevitable.

Since your goal is to keep squireels away from the birds' feed, let us look at a number of methods. Hang or post mount the feeder at least twenty feet from the nearest tree and six or more feet above the ground. The post should be slick metal. You can incorporate conical or disk-shaped baffles at least four feet up the post or on any wires used to hang the feeder. Any other barriers you incorporate into your design should be made of metal or tough plastic to prevent squirrels from chewing through them.

As a last, or even preventive resort, you can offer cracked corn or whole cobs of dried corn to distract squirrels away from the more expensive seeds intended for song birds mounted higher up. The corn can be dispensed on the ground or up in trees. Cobs of dried corn can even be spiked onto propellor-like squirrel feeders mounted on trees that keep squirrels occuped while providing humans with goofy entertainment. You may even find that squirrels are just as much fun to watch as most birds.

# Predator Barriers

Birds will be much more able to experience the peaceful enjoyment of your feeder, house or bath if you install physical barriers to prevent the inevitable harassment of unwanted guests. These barriers are particularly effective against four-legged intruders.

Poles, posts and trees can be fitted with a sleeve of aluminum sheeting that will defy the traction of claws. It must be installed at least five feet above ground level. If you have a metal pole, it wouldn't hurt to grease it.

Conical foils can be constructed out of aluminum sheeting to fit both round and square posts. Join and attach the assembly with self-tapping sheet metal screws, which can be installed with an electric drill. Position the foil at least four feet above ground level.

If your bird structure is suspended, use heavy wire instead of rope. Squirrels can climb down and gnaw through rope. You can also install metal pie pans as baffles on the wire to foil dauntless intruders. The wire can be attached to another wire spanning two trees or man-made structures, but a feeder should be at least twenty feet from a tree or other tall structure to be out of jumping range.

Yet another way to impede cats is to spread chicken wire just above the ground beneath a feeder or house. This will compromise their ability to leap because they will be unable to build up speed on the ground.

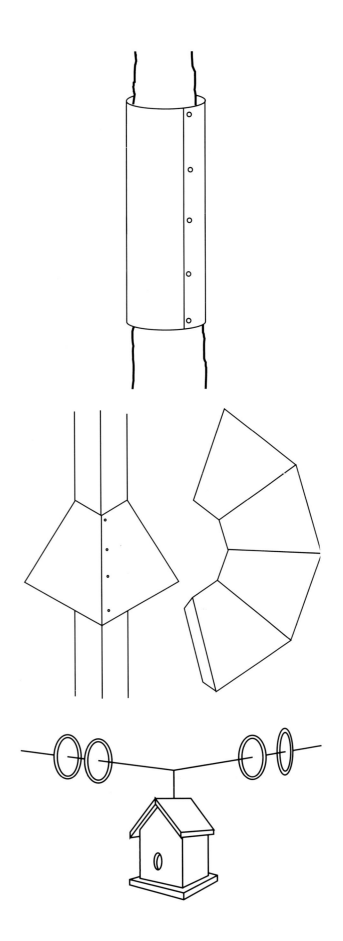

# Mounting

Most birds will probably prefer houses that are firmly mounted on a post, tree or wall. Yet this does not rule out hanging, especially for feeders. Observe all siting specifications before planning how you will mount your structure.

If you hang something from a tree, wrap the branch with fabric or inner tube rubber where you attach the wire to prevent damage to the tree. Make sure the branch is strong enough to support the structure.

When mounting a house or feeder to the trunk of a tree, it is preferable to use a batten. This is a vertical plank, almost twice as high as the structure, which reduces the stress from the protruding center of gravity. Use galvanized screws, or a strong strap around the trunk, to attach the batten to the tree. Use galvanized hardware also when attaching a structure to a wall.

Posts can be metal or wooden. Use pressure treated lumber or cedar, whether square or round. Sink the post at least 18" using a post hole digger. Add gravel at the bottom for wood. Concrete isn't necessary, but pack the dirt well around the shaft. The top of a metal pipe can be threaded to fit a floor flange attached to the base of your bird structure. Wooden posts can be reinforced with metal L-brackets or wooden triangular braces at the top.

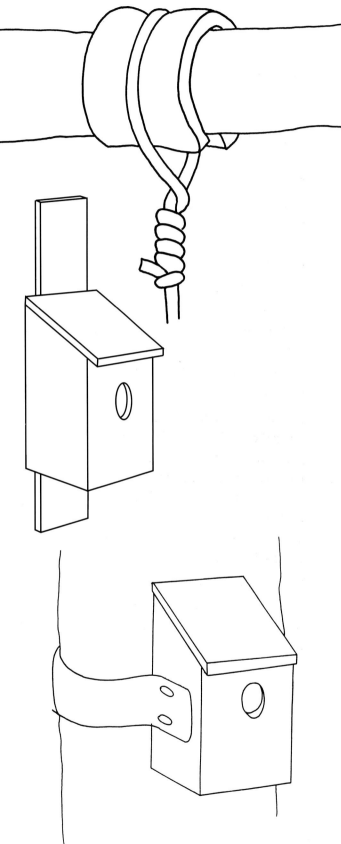

# Siting

There are several things to consider when choosing an appropriate site for your feeder, house or bath. You will want to create an environment that is especially attractive to birds. Providing food, water and shelter is a good beginning. Placing these near trees, shrubs and flowers is another way to enhance a bird habitat. You should emphasize any of these elements which might usually be missing in the surrounding area. For instance, on the plains, introduce trees. In the desert, provide water. During winter, display food.

Birds prefer border habitat like where an open meadow or lawn meets the edge of a grove of trees. This allows unobstructed access and egress while maintaining proximity to food, nesting materials and safe haven in the forest.

Feeders can be moved gradually closer to your house as birds get accustomed to using them. This will give you better views of the birds from your window. In fact, some feeders are designed for placement directly at your window for optimum viewing.

Orient the entry hole of a house away from prevailing wind-driven rain. To attract the more timid birds, houses and feeders should face away from the activity of people, such as sidewalks, driveways and children's play areas. Avoid sites that receive extreme sunshine. For the more open nesting boxes and platforms, a sheltered and reasonably hidden site is preferable. Refer to the chart on pages 14 and 15 for more specific site requirements.

If your yard lacks the appropriate vegetation, consider some creative landscaping to attract birds to your habitat. For instance, pyracantha has beautiful berries that birds love in winter months. Sunflowers are another sure bet. See what you can grow in your area.

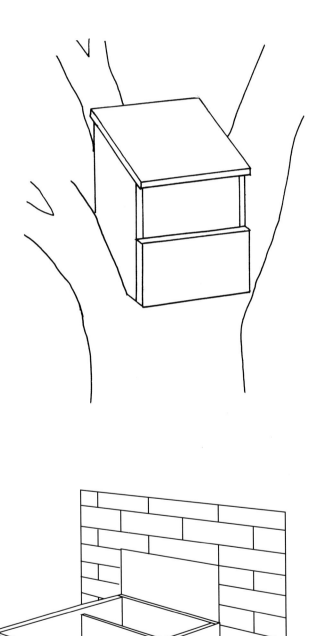

# Construction Basics

## Materials

There are no ideal materials for building bird feeders and houses. Moisture will eventually take its toll in the form of rot and rust, even undermining glue joints and finishes. Other factors such as sunshine, temperature fluctuation, toxic chemical components, expense and availability must also figure in to your choice of materials. Let's examine the most likely options.

**Solid Wood** is still a favorite choice, being both aesthetic and easy to work with. One disadvantage, however, is that it's commercially available only in 3/4" and greater thicknesses. If you have access to a thickness planer, this can be remedied. Otherwise you may encounter limitations having to incorporate such thick boards in your miniaturized designs. Another shortcoming of conventional lumber is the knots and other flaws that can complicate the assembly of small structures. It's worth the small extra expense to purchase the higher grades of lumber.

Many of the designs in this book call for pine, but you should feel free to substitute more rot-resistant or elegant species wherever you choose. These include cedar, redwood, cypress, and various tropical woods like banak. Locally you may find yew, black locust, fruitwoods and others. Western cedar is widely available and inexpensive, but its aroma may keep some birds such as chickadees from nesting in houses made of it. Clear-heart redwood is great to work with, but it costs at least twice as much as cedar. If you want to mix woods, be aware that stock thicknesses between species usually vary slightly, which can complicate accurate joinery.

Even though pressure-treated wood is rot-resistant, it should be avoided, except as mounting posts. The chromated copper arsenate with which it is treated doesn't belong with bird feed or tiny nestlings.

**Plywood** offers several practical advantages. It is strong, unlikely to warp, inexpensive and available in many dimensions. Of the many types, only marine- or exterior-grade plywood and oriented strand board are recommended for bird structures. The others either lack weather resistance or contain toxic substances. Still, with any plywood, care must be taken to seal any exposed end grain against weather.

Marine plywood is superior in that it has no voids, even in the inner laminations. Exterior plywoods are graded by letters which indicate the quality of both faces. For bird structures, use A-C or B-C, and face the better surface outward. Oriented strand board, not to be confused with particle or flake board, is all the same grade. Each of these plywoods is available in standard thicknesses of 1/4", 3/8", 1/2" and 3/4".

**Plastics** offer some unique possibilities. Tube feeders utilize PVC or clear plastic cylinders. Plexiglass is preferable to glass when used as windows in hopper feeders. Plastic sheeting can be curved and bent with heat, cut with fine-tooth blades, and joined with glues and bolts to form durable structures.

**Adhesives** usually need to be reinforced with nails or screws. Yellow carpenter's glue lacks water resistance but holds adequately when under roof and reinforced with metal fasteners. Two-part epoxy is expensive but sometimes necessary to bind critical junctures where no other fasteners can be used. Clear silicone caulk is quite effective in both sealing and adhering. A hot-melt glue gun is a handy tool for making waterproof seals, though the glue has relatively low adhesive strength.

**Fasteners** should always be corrosion-resistant. Nails and screws should be galvanized steel, stainless steel, or brass. Hinges, latches or other hardware that is exposed should never be plated. Use solid stainless, aluminum or brass.

**Finishes** are actually used on wood more for structural and aesthetic reasons than to protect it from weathering. Unsealed wood expands and contracts as it exchanges moisture with the atmosphere, thus stressing the joints. Heat affects this process unevenly since only certain areas are exposed to sunlight, causing more stress. Even so, structural considerations need not overrule your appreciation for the beauty of naturally weathered wood. The small seams of bird structures will usually withstand these stresses.

Stains will help seal the wood while enhancing its look. A clear top finish can also be added, but must be compatible with the stain. Alkyd stains are oil based. Acrylic stains are water based, easier to apply and clean up, and longer lasting. Clear coatings include polyurethane, marine spar varnish, and penetrating oils which need to be reapplied every year or so. Exterior-rated primers and paints work well, but avoid those which contain mercury.

Any finish you apply must cover all surfaces of the wood, once all glue seams are dry. Pay close attention to all exposed end grain, especially on plywood. Let the structure dry thoroughly at least two weeks or until no odor lingers before letting birds use it.

Concerning the dimensions given in the materials lists, 1 x 12 is a stock size for dressed lumber which actually measures 3/4" x 11-1/4", whereas 1" x 12" means just that. Watch for the inch ( " ) marks. Also, the exact dimensions of a finished component may not always be listed, but the stock needed to make the part is listed.

# Tools and Techniques

The projects in this book cover a rather wide range of difficulty. A child can make some, while others require an experienced woodworker. Most, however, are very manageable for anyone with moderate craft skills. In fact, building small-scale projects such as these is a wonderful and inexpensive way to develop your talents. You may soon become inspired to design your own.

Many of the projects require only simple hand tools: hammer, screw drivers, saws and a crank drill. Other tools will be required for specific projects: whittling knife, side cutters, pliers, files or chisels. A power drill and a coping saw will come in handy. All sorts of power tools will improve efficiency and accuracy if you have them, but are not absolutely necessary: jigsaw, hole saw, band saw, planers, routers, etc. However, a table saw is more or less required for about half the projects.

Most of the joinery used throughout these bird structures involves butt joints. Although they are the weakest of all joints, they are quite adequate for small structures, especially when properly glued, nailed and reinforced by other intersecting boards. Miter joints involve two beveled edges butting together, such as roof peaks, wall corners and molding that trims corners. Gluing is crucial since fasteners will not hold as well as with butt joints. However, miter joints seal all the end grain and present a neater appearance. Dado joints include several variations

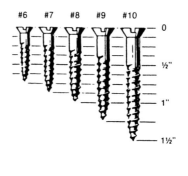

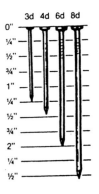

and are rarely used here. They generally require a table saw and are quite strong when accurately fit. Dado grooves are used for movable panels as well as the sort of multiple partitions found in martin houses.

To create a strong glue joint, there should be a minimum of gaps between the adjoining pieces. Cuts should be made smoothly and evenly, and the pieces should be held together tightly until the glue has dried. Good gluing technique is especially important for plywood, since fasteners won't hold well in the laminated grain. Always use plenty of glue for maximum seam strength. Excess can be wiped away after clamping, unless you plan to use stain, a clear finish or to leave wood unfinished. In that case, use just enough glue spread inside the joint without squirting and dripping outside the seams. Trim away any excess *after* glue has dried using a knife and sandpaper.

Screws hold better than nails but are compromised when penetrating end grain, and nearly useless in plywood endgrain. Unless the wood is very soft or the screws are very slender, holes should be pre-drilled to a diameter slightly smaller than the screws being inserted. You might also consider using corrosion-resistant threaded nails, but only for permanent joints since they cannot be removed.

To cut small entry holes in solid wood, a power drill with a spade bit can be used. A hole saw works nicely for larger holes and for plywood. A coping saw can be used if you lack a hole saw. A coping saw or jigsaw is also useful for cutting square holes or scroll cuts. Use fine-tooth blades and cut so that the non-splintering side is on the good face. Saw with patience and don't force the blade.

When joining walls to a floor or base, where water may collect, cut the wall panels so that their grain runs parallel to the base. End grain will then meet vertically at the corners rather than butting against the floor where water can wick up and increase rot.

*Important:* Be careful to read all of the instructions to understand a project before beginning to make it.

And finally, some important tips on safety. Operate all power tools with special care. Familiarize yourself with any appropriate safety techniques such as push sticks, jigs and feather sticks. Always wear eye protection and a dust mask when cutting or sanding. Ventilate your work space properly. Use common sense, and if you're unsure about something, don't try it. If you're tired, stop.

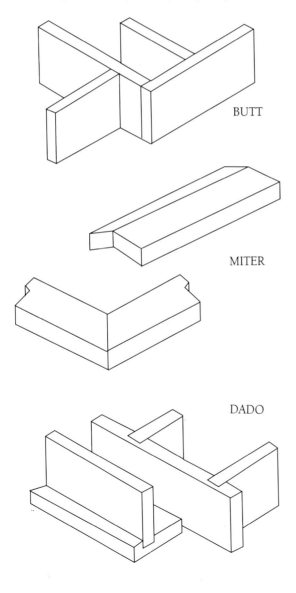

BUTT

MITER

DADO

# Feeding Habits

Birds have high energy needs due to very high metabolic rates, especially the smaller species. They must eat the equivalent of between 40 and 75 percent of their body weight each day just to survive. Humans can play a very beneficial role in supplementing bird diets, particularly during severe weather such as droughts or prolonged snow cover.

The best time to start feeding birds is in early autumn. Certain flocks, like chickadees and juncos, will actually make their winter homes around good feeding areas. Because many birds will start to rely on the feed you put out, it is important to maintain your feeding program through the winter. If you must leave for awhile, taper off gradually or, better yet, ask a neighbor to take over while you're away. Come spring, providing feed is optional since natural food sources become abundant once again. There's no need to fear that birds will abandon wild foods just because they visit your feeder regularly. Providing water is a good year-round practice, though most critical during extremely cold weather.

There's not very much you can do to exclude ruffian starlings or gangs of sparrows in favor of the prettier songbirds. The best solution is to offer something to all. Set up a few different kinds of feeders, spaced apart, each with a different menu. Fill your feeders early to attract small birds like titmice, since starlings and blue jays eat later in the day. Sparrows often avoid hanging feeders. A ground feeder with inexpensive cracked corn, mixed seed or table scraps will divert many larger birds from the more expensive seed in elevated feeders.

**Seeds** are the most popular of feeds used to stock feeders. Although birds enjoy a great variety of seeds, which can even be mixed to suit the species in your area, sunflower seeds are the favorite of most birds. Chances are you live in a climate where you can grow your own sunflowers.

**Nuts** are also popular. Almost any kind will be eaten by birds, but unsalted peanuts are best. They can be strung up in their shells, mixed with other nuts in mesh bag feeders, or sprinkled almost anywhere. You'll enjoy watching nuthatches, titmice and downy woodpeckers perform their antics to get nuts hung right at your window.

**Suet** is hard fat trimmed from the kidneys and loins of beef or lamb. Birds love it plain during the cold months. For summer it can be rendered into "bird cakes." Melt small pieces in a pan and pour it over seeds, nuts, dried fruit, or almost any bird food, and let it cool. Or, try this alternative recipe: combine in a blender 1 part vegetable shortening, 1 part peanut butter, 1 part flour, 1 part cracked corn and 3 parts yellow corn meal. Insect-eating birds eat suet in winter when insects are scarce.

**Cereal and Grain** products are suitable when soaked or crumbled up for small beaks. Oats, breads, cakes, cookies, pastries, corn flakes and other variations appeal to birds.

**Fruits and Vegetables** such as dried peas and lentils can be served. Dried fruits such as currants and sultanas are favored by many species. Try a shish-kabob of apple, orange and other fruits to further delight bird palates.

**Animal Products** like small tidbits of meat, bones and cheese, along with other kitchen scraps are also worthy of bird consumption. There's almost no limit to supplementing a bird's diet.

When you opt for seed, buy in bulk. Store it in clean, dry containers with lids. Find a scoop to load your feeder, perhaps a plastic pitcher or milk jug with its bottom cut out. Clean your feeder periodically with hot water and mild detergent. Keep all feeding stations clear of old food scraps that rot and attract rats, causing infection and disease.

# Feeder Fillers

**White Proso Millet:** Cardinals, Cowbirds, Finches (House, Chaffinch, Green Finch), Mourning Doves, Redpolls (Common), Sparrows (Field, House, White-throated), Wrens (Carolina)

**Fine Cracked Corn:** Blue Jays, Cardinals, Grosbeaks (Evening and Rose-breasted), Sparrows (Field, House, and others), Towhees (Green-tailed, Spotted, and Rufous-sided)

**Black Oil Sunflower:** American Goldfinches, Cardinals, Chickadees (Black-capped and Carolina), Grosbeaks (Evening and Rose-breasted), Grackles (Common), Finches (House and Purple), Mourning Doves, Sparrows (Field, House, Chipping, and White-throated)

**Black Striped Sunflower:** Blue Jays, Cardinals, Chickadees (Black-capped and Carolina), Grosbeaks (Evening and Red-Breasted), Grackles (Common), Finches (House and Purple), Titmice (Tufted), Mourning Doves, Sparrows (House and White-throated)

**Hulled Raw Sunflower:** Mourning Doves, Sparrows (House)

**Niger (Thistle):** American Goldfinches, Finches (House and Purple), Mourning Doves

**Safflower:** Cardinals

**Raw Peanuts:** Blue Jays, Chickadees (Black-capped and Carolina), Finches (House, Green and Purple), Goldfinches (American), Grackles (Common), Grosbeaks (Evening and Rose-breasted), Juncos, Nuthatches (Red- and White-breasted), Sparrows (Field, House and White-throated), Titmice (Tufted), Wrens (Carolina)

**Suet:** Blue Birds, Cardinals, Crows, Chickadees (Black-capped and Carolina), Coal tits, Flickers, Goldfinches, Jackdaws, Juncos, Kinglets, Nuthatches (Red- and White-breasted), Thrushes, Titmice (Tufted), Warblers, Woodpeckers (Downy, Hairy, Red-bellied, Red-headed), Wrens

**Fruit Slices:** Blackbirds, Bluetits, Catbirds, Fieldfares, Orioles (Baltimore, Orchard, Spotted), Redwings, Robins (English), Tanagers (Scarlet, Summer, Western)

**Hemp Seed:** Finches (House, Chaffinch, Green Finch), Tits, Pipits

# Wild Feeds

**Wood Duck:** Acorns, beech nuts, water plants

**American Kestrel:** Mainly insects, small mammals, reptiles

**Northern Bobwhite:** Seeds

**California Quail:** Seeds

**Dove:** Grass seeds, other seeds, and grains

**Barn Owl:** Rodents

**Great Horned Owl:** Skunks, rats, squirrels, grouse, weasels, snakes and insects

**Eastern Screech Owl:** Worms, crayfish, mice, small birds, insects

**Chimney Swift:** Flying insects

**Hummingbird:** Flower nectar, tree sap, some insects

**Woodpecker:** Acorns and other tree fruit; some insects

**Flicker:** Ants, insects, berries

**Eastern Kingbird:** Insects

**Eastern Phoebe:** Mainly insects

**Least Flycatcher:** Insects

**Swallow:** Mainly insects

**Purple Martin:** Insects

**Blue Jay:** Acorns, beech nuts, tree mast, insects, birds' eggs, nestlings, voles and mice

**Black-billed Magpie:** Insects, seeds, berries, eggs, mice, carrion

**Crow:** Animals, vegetables

**Tufted Titmouse:** Mainly insects; also seeds and berries

**Bushtit and Chickadee:** Mainly insects; seeds and berries

**Eastern Bluebird:** Insects; also berries, fruit and seeds

**Western Bluebird:** Insects, spiders, invertebrates; berries

**Thrush:** Insects, invertebrates, berries and seeds

**Brown Creeper:** Insects; seeds

**Nuthatch:** Insects, spiders, nuts, seeds and berries

**Wren:** Insects, invertebrates; sometimes seeds

**Blue-gray Gnatcatcher:** Mainly insects; other invertebrates

**Kinglet:** Insects, spiders and some berries

**Robin:** Earthworms, grubs, larvae, insects, spiders; berries, fruit, seeds

**Cardinal:** Mainly seeds and fruit; also insects and spiders

**Mockingbird:** Wild berries, seeds, insects and invertebrates

**Brown Thrasher:** Insects, small invertebrates, some fruit and seeds

**Cedar Waxwing:** Mainly berries and seeds; also insects

**Warbler:** Mainly insects and spiders; sometimes seeds and berries

**Yellowthroat:** Insects

**American Redstart:** Insects, spiders, fruit and seeds

**Grosbeak:** Insects and fruit; seeds and berries

**Bunting:** Insects, spiders, berries and seeds

**Towhee:** Seeds, fruit and insects

**Dark-eyed Junco:** Mainly insects and seeds

**Finch:** Mainly seeds and fruit; also insects

**Oriole:** Mainly insects and spiders; also fruit and seeds

**Brown-headed Cowbird:** Grain, seeds, berries and other fruit; some insects

**Common Grackle:** Insects, grass seeds, worms, eggs and young birds

**Eastern Meadowlark:** Insects, grubs, grass and weed seeds

**Blackbird:** Insects and seeds

**Sparrow:** Insects, seeds and fruit

**Red Crossbill:** Pine seeds, other fruit and seeds

**Pine Siskin:** Seeds and some insects

**Common Redpoll:** Mainly insects and fruit

**A Versatile Mix:** White proso millet, fine cracked corn, and black oil sunflower (see birds for the next three listings)

**White Proso Millet:** Cardinals, Cowbirds, Finches (House, Chaffinch, Green Finch), Mourning Doves, Redpolls (Common), Sparrows (Field, House, White-throated), Wrens (Carolina)

**Fine Cracked Corn:** Blue Jays, Cardinals, Grosbeaks (Evening and Rose-Breasted), Sparrows (Field, House, and others), Towhees (Green-tailed, Spotted, and Rufous-sided)

**Black Oil Sunflower:** American Goldfinches, Cardinals, Chickadees (Black-capped and Carolina), Grosbeaks (Evening and Rose-breasted), Grackles (Common), Finches (House and Purple), Mourning Doves, Sparrows (Field, House, Chipping, and White-throated)

**Black Striped Sunflower:** Blue Jays, Cardinals, Chickadees (Black-capped and Carolina), Grosbeaks (Evening and Red-breasted), Grackles (Common), Finches (House and Purple), Titmice (Tufted), Mourning Doves, Sparrows (House and White-throated)

**Hulled Raw Sunflower:** Mourning Doves, Sparrows (House)

# Feeder-Fillers

Just as bird house design can be used to attract (or exclude) specific species, your feeder's fare can be planned to suit the birds you'd most like to observe.

When trying to cater to birds not listed below, your best guide is the beak shape. A bird's bill is the key to its diet. Note the heavy, seed-cracking beaks of cardinals and finches; the insect-probes of the robin, woodpecker and (most dramatically) woodcock; and the multi-purpose bill of the opportunistic star-

**A Versatile Mix**

**White Proso Millet**

**Fine Cracked Corn**

**Black Oil Sunflower**

**Black Striped Sunflower**

**Hulled Raw Sunflower**

# that Fowl Favor

ling. Use these clues to suit your feeder's menu to the patrons you'd most like to attract.

And then, once you've earned a regular clientele, be sure to keep the feeder stocked. Especially in the cold months, when natural sources of food are not available, the sudden shutdown of a feeding station can leave birds stranded, foodless, and in a spot that, were it not for the accustomed bounty of the feeder, they would never have frequented.

**Niger (Thistle)**

**Safflower**

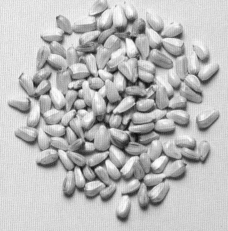

**Raw Peanuts**

**Suet**

**Fruit Slices**

**Hemp Seed**

**Niger (Thistle):** American Goldfinches, Finches (House and Purple), Mourning Doves

**Safflower:** Cardinals

**Raw Peanuts:** Blue Jays, Chickadees (Black-capped and Carolina), Finches (House, Green and Purple), Goldfinches (American), Grackles (Common), Grosbeaks (Evening and Rose-breasted), Juncos, Nuthatches (Red- and White-breasted), Sparrows (Field, House and White-Throated), Titmice (Tufted), Wrens (Carolina)

**Suet:** Blue Birds, Cardinals, Crows, Chickadees (Black-capped and Carolina), Coal tits, Flickers, Goldfinches, Jackdaws, Juncos, Kinglets, Nuthatches (Red- and White-breasted), Thrushes, Titmice (Tufted), Warblers, Woodpeckers (Downy, Hairy, Red-bellied, Red-headed), Wrens

**Fruit Slices:** Blackbirds, Bluetits, Catbirds, Fieldfares, Orioles (Baltimore, Orchard, Spotted), Redwings, Robins (English), Tanagers (Scarlet, Summer, Western)

**Hemp Seed:** Finches (House, Chaffinch, Green Finch), Tits, Pipits

*"Everyone Needs a Home"* (series) by
Don Bundrick

*"Boyds in the 'Hood"* by Don Bundrick

# Gallery

*"Cross Birdhouses"* (series) by Charles Ratliff

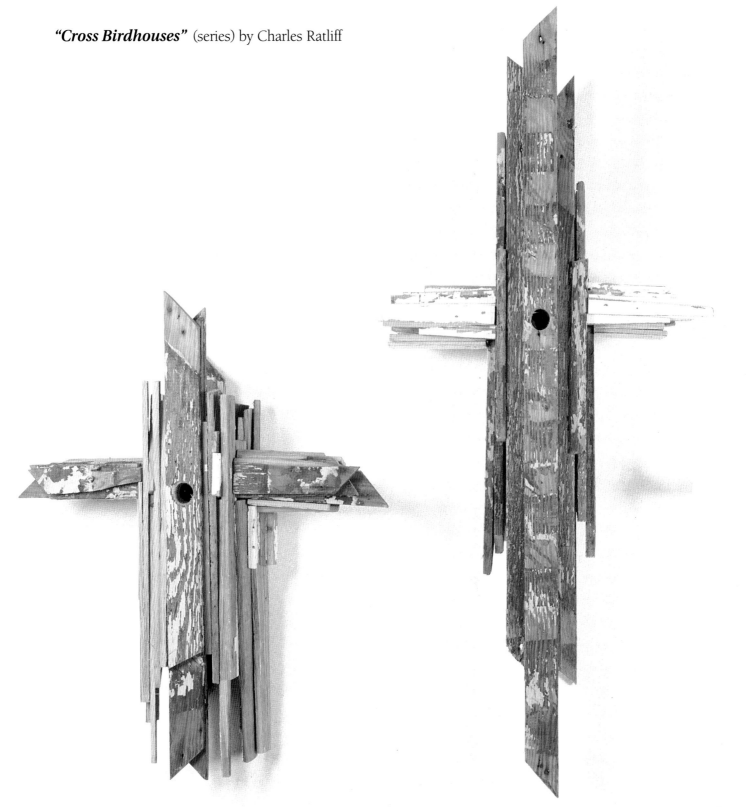

# Gallery

Three *"Gourd Houses"* by Harold Hall

Opposite, *"Lighthouse"* by Fox Watson & the students at Juvenile Evaluation Center, Swannanoa, NC

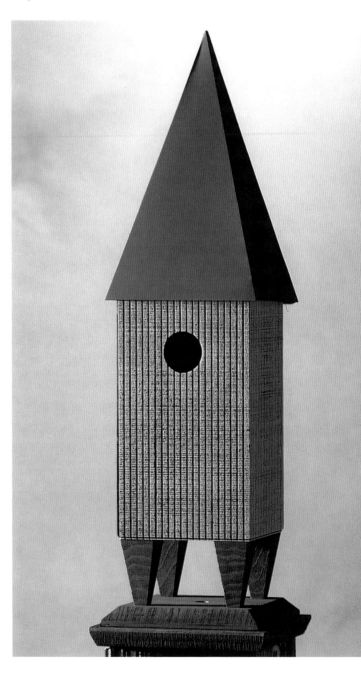

*"Bluebird House"*
by Paul Sumner

Three *"Nuthatch Houses"* by Paul Sumner

***Bird Houses*** by Susan Starr

*"Standing Birdhouse"* by Bryant Holsenbeck

*"A-Frame Birdhouse"* (front and back views) by Bobby Hansson

***Bird Houses*** by Barry Leader

**Bird Baths** by Debra Fritts
(Photos by Sue Ann Kuhn-Smith)

*"If That Mockingbird Don't Sing"* (left and detail) and *"Nature Gets The Exxit"* (middle) by Mana D. C. Hewitt

**"Closed Doors"** (open and closed)
by Mana D. C. Hewitt

**"Global View"** (open and closed)
by Mana D. C. Hewitt

**"Ironclad Monitor"** by Randy Sewell

**"Tar Paper Fishing Shack"**
by Randy Sewell

**"Oasis"** by Randy Sewell

***"Radio World"***
by Randy Sewell

***"Java Jive"*** by Randy Sewell

***"Silo Birdfeeder"***
by Randy Sewell

***"Lewis' Reptile Farm"***
by Randy Sewell

LEWIS' REPTILE FARM

THIS IS IT    LIZARDS    SNAKES    SEE

GIFT SHOP - ICE

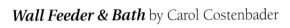

***Wall Feeder & Bath*** by Carol Costenbader

***Amorphous Environ*** by David Renfroe

***"Sunflower Birdhouse"*** by West Olive Folk Art

***"Country Bird Feeder"***
by Bruce Malicoat

# Twig Tent Feeder

What could be more simple—an A-frame roof over a feeding platform. The materials and construction may vary, but they're all within reach and easy to assemble. This is a great way to start feeding—and watching—birds.

*These two rustic creations from Garden Source illustrate how elaborate facades can embellish livable bird chambers (see page 66 for basic construction techniques).*

*Artful bird houses exhibited at the Wustum Museum in Racine, Wisconsin.*

**While not included in the instructional section of this book, bird houses such as these transcend functionalism, achieving the status of fine art.**

*The aspiring bird house builder can find inspiration in these four functional designs by Randy Sewell, suitable for post-mounting.*

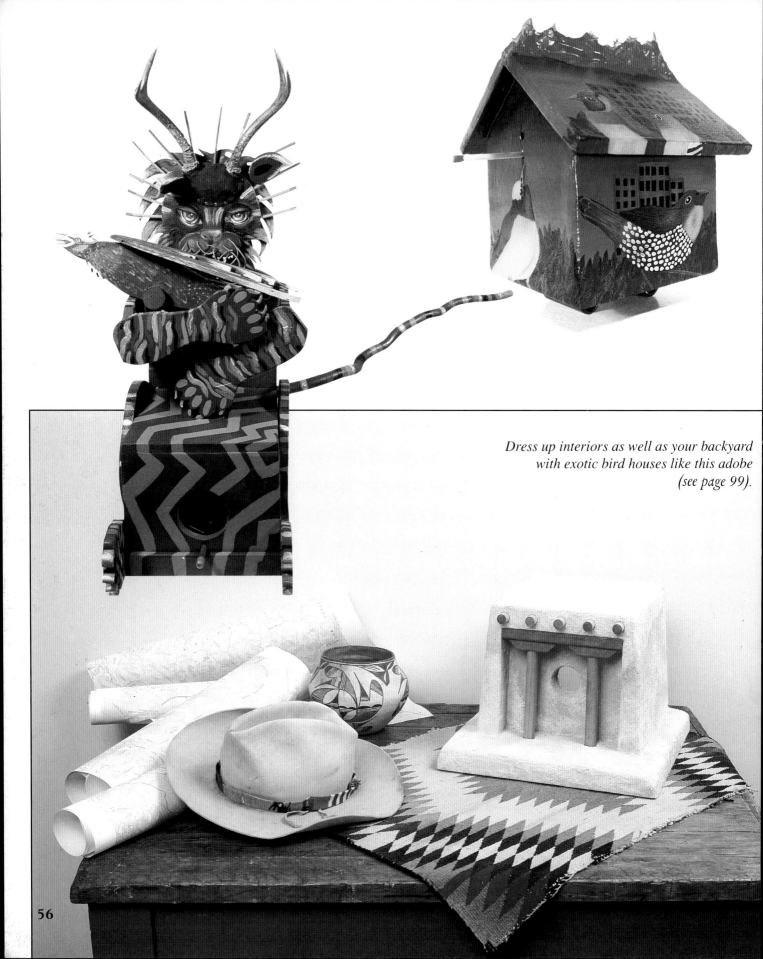

*Dress up interiors as well as your backyard
with exotic bird houses like this adobe
(see page 99).*

# The BIRD HOUSES

# Gourds

If you've been wondering what good gourds are, ask a purple martin. Now that we've invented synthetic bowls and cups, gourds are seldom used for much other than ornamentation. That's a shame, because they offer ideal bird quarters.

There's little to say about building a gourd bird house. Just drill an appropriate-size hole with a hole saw. But there's a bit more to say about the creative possibilities of Nature's own bird house.

Gourds invite decoration—Southwestern pueblo, as we chose, or even more natural motifs. But there's more.

Gourds grow readily anywhere pumpkins and squash thrive. Consider planting your own suburb. They like a deep, well-drained soil (not too much fertilizer; they'll over-produce foliage). Gourds can actually be molded as they're grown. With careful bending by hand or with tape, you may find a pink flamingo and other exotics hiding in your garden.

The Titmouse

*Gourd houses are easily hung in trees, and prove to be quite attractive when painted.*

# Thatched Gourd House

Birds may have to evict the gnomes before setting up housekeeping in this elfin-looking abode. Either way, you'll enjoy hanging this enchanting shelter in your yard.

## Materials List

*Pear-shaped gourd*
*Spare gourd*
*Broom corn*
*2' Raffia*
*Glue*

**Step One** Select a medium-sized, pear-shaped gourd that is tapered downward to a flat bottom. Drill a 1-1/4" hole in the side of the gourd for an entrance hole. Carefully clean out the seeds. A piece of coat hanger with a small hook on one end is helpful in the cleaning process. Cut off the stem and use it for a perch, gluing it into a pre-drilled hole.

**Step Two** If you decide to stain your gourd, do so now. Add a coat of clear acrylic after the stain and glue have dried.

**Step Three** The roof is made from broom corn stalks cut to about 3"–4". Most craft stores carry broom corn. Three layers, glued progressively higher up the gourd, should be enough. You can use a hot glue gun to attach the rows of broom corn.

**Step Four** The porch roof is cut from the neck of another gourd and glued on. Since the apex of the roof will look ragged from the tips of the broom corn, a cap should be made from the top of another gourd and glued securely on top.

**Step Five** The thatch is held in place with a band of some natural material like raffia. Dried flowers would add a nice touch, tucked through the raffia band.

# Acorn Gourd House

Gourds make wonderful bird houses. Different ways of cultivating various species add to the design possibilities. Hang this giant acorn from your tallest oak.

## Materials List

*Dipper gourd*
*Bottle gourd*

**Step One** Select a medium-sized dipper gourd with a tapered bottom for the chamber. Cut off the neck of the gourd at a point just above the largest part of the ball, and clean out the seeds. Save the stem to use for the perch.

**Step Two** Drill an entrance hole about 1-1/4" dia., or start with a sampler hole and enlarge it using sandpaper wrapped around a pencil. Drill a smaller hole just big enough to accept a piece of the gourd stem for a perch.

**Step Three** Select a bottle gourd of the same size but with a flatter bottom for the acorn's cap. Cut this gourd just below the widest point. Use the bottom piece for the cap. Drill a small hole in the center of this part.

Insert the stem as the stem of the acorn.

**Step Four** Fit the cap over the house section and glue them together. Wood burning or painting the cap to look like a real acorn cap will be effective for a natural look. Wood stains of different hues will also enhance the bird house. When you are satisfied with the look you've achieved, spray with a clear coat of acrylic finish.

# Split-Log House

When you've had your fill of the confines of the workshop and the precision of cabinetmaking, you might enjoy woodworking on a cruder scale. Crank up the chainsaw, head for the woods, and get back to basics.

The house could either be attached directly to a tree, to close up the back, or you could add a board to the back to seal the chamber. The latter approach gives you more mounting options, but the house is really at its best in full camouflage.

Find a straight-grained log about 8" diameter, and cut a 12" cross-section—with one end square and the other on a slant. Next, rip about a 2" slab off square to the sloping end, removing the longer side. This cut needs to be as square and flat as possible. (The trick here is to keep the log from moving while you saw; wedge it between other logs. Also, you'll probably have better luck if you keep the angle of the bar to the length of the log small. The saw will cut better, and more of the bar will be in the wood, helping keep the cut straight.)

With that done, remove 2" from each end, making the cuts as square and clean as you're able. (If you have a band saw, use it!) Save these two cutoffs. The sloping end will be reattached as the roof, and the square one will become the floor.

Now it's time to remove a 4" wide, 4" deep chamber from the heart of the log. Set the 8" section flat, with its rounded side down, and make five 4"-deep incisions lengthwise and about an inch apart in the flat face. Then put the chainsaw away, and get comfortable with a large (at least 1") chisel and a mallet. (Here's where you find out how good you are at judging straight grain from the outside.) Work your way down with the chisel through the 1" sections left by the saw cuts until you've hollowed out a 4"-deep, 4"-wide chamber.

Use a 1-1/4" (for house wrens) or 1-1/2" (for Bewick's, Carolina, and other wrens) bit to bore a hole into the middle of the chamber. Then, at your option, bore a smaller hole below to insert a piece of dowel for a perch.

All that's left is to reattach the top and bottom (drilling lead holes for 16d galvanized nails so the wood won't split). If you did a tidy job removing them, the cut lines shouldn't be very obvious.

The Three-Toed Woodpecker

Sawmill leavings make great raw material for avian contractors. You may have seen bird houses and feeders resembling these before, and wondered where the builders got those lovely boards with the bark left on. Answer: by the ton from a sawmill. When the board factory squares up a log, slabs are left—useful only to wood burners, and the artisan with an eye for found materials.

*Picky Bird Panacea*

*Rustic houses are particularly well-suited to species that are picky about the spaces they'll inhabit. You may have better luck attracting woodpeckers and wood ducks, for example, if you build them a bark-faced or log house of suitable dimensions.*

# Construction

Should you have a source for bark-on slabs, you ought to try working with them. The single flat surface doesn't lend itself to the conventional geometry of woodworking but leaves many opportunities for inventive techniques.

A few guidelines: the most popular bark-faced slabs are birch (in the northeast), poplar (in the southeast), and pine (elsewhere). They are readily available, and the birch has a particularly attractive bark. As the layer of wood right below the bark (the sapwood) in these species dries, it will shrink and tend to pull away from the bark. If you drive your nails through the bark and into the solid wood, things will hang together better down the road. Wherever possible, try to give the end grain a little protection by covering it with small branches.

Other than that, these dwellings ought to be free-form art. Let the materials inspire you which direction to go.

To create the twig-faced house, start with a basic box—even a store-bought item will serve admirably. Then visit your backyard or a nearby field to select your building materials. Look for straight bushes, water shoots, grasses, vines, and other colorful vegetation that is dry and has firmly attached bark (or, remove the bark). In any regrown section of disturbed ground, you should be able to find a vivid selection of browns, greens, yellows, and even reds among the underbrush.

Back at home, arm yourself with a hot-melt glue gun, a small hand saw, a utility knife, and pruning shears, and begin cutting and attaching twigs to the front of the house. Remember that the lengths of wood should overlap the ones that will be attached to the sides. Leave extra length, which can be trimmed later.

Our house capitalizes on subtle geometric patterns accentuated by color changes, all of which is visually broken by the twist of red-berried vine around the hole. On the roof are dried grasses held in place by lengths of wisteria attached to the top with 4d galvanized nails. The options are, of course, as boundless as your sources and your imagination.

# Old Crows' Tavern

**If you wanted a vintage bottle of wine, would you buy this year's pickings and wait? Of course not. Likewise here, where the builders sought the appearance of an aging—should we say moldering?—backroad watering hole.**

And what better source of that look could there be than old building materials? Faced with sections of driftwood board and capped with old sheet metal, this is actually a conventional wooden bird house beneath. The interior dimensions of that inner box and the diameter of the entry hole could be set to suit a number of smaller nesting birds, though this example is best suited to wrens or chickadees.

Barn wood may be the most readily available material for building new old bird houses. The more weathered and cracked, the better. A few tips, though: watch out for nails, which are hard to spot when rusted but still perfectly capable of ruining a saw; use a coarse rip blade to leave saw marks on the wood for authenticity; and plan on ending up with a dull saw blade, as old wood gets very hard.

Proper painting is just as important as the material it's applied to. Try thinning flat white paint and rubbing it on with a cloth or sponge. Use a dry cloth to smudge off corners to achieve a worn look. Black paint can be used in a similar way to good effect on the roof and for windows.

As is the case with nearly every project in this book, the point is inspiration, not imitation. Scrounge around to see what you can find. Why, even the nails could be recycled.

The Crow

# Log Cabin

## MATERIALS LIST

(2) 1 x 8 x 8-3/4" Pine
(2) 1 x 3" x 7" Pine
(4) 3/4" x 4' Dowels
3/4" x 3' Dowels
3/8" x 2" x 3" Plywood
(2) 3/8 x 1" x 3" Plywood
1 x 3/4" x 4" Pine
1 x 8 x 7" Pine
(2) 1 x 8 x 11" Pine
1 x 2 x 2-1/2" Pine
1/4" x 1" Dowels
6d Galvanized finish nails
8d Galvanized finish nails
(4) 3/16" x 4" steel rods

### Toy Houses

*Another attractive and entertaining approach to building log bird houses is to use one of the many toy construction sets, fitting the pieces with glue and small nails for permanence. You could end up with positively presidential accommodations.*

**To tell the truth, this pioneering approach to bird lodgings is a log house in appearance only. Much simpler to construct than some twig amalgam, our pine box achieves the traditional look with a facade fashioned of halved 3/4" dowels, while retaining the virtues of solid lumber's strength and weather-resistance. Not only is it fun to look at, you'll also be entertained by this project's uncanny use of materials.**

Start by sawing the 8-3/4"-long front and back walls from 1 x 8 stock. Then connect points 4" up each 7-1/4" side with one in the center of the 8-3/4" top. Create the roof peak by sawing along these lines (the angle is about 37°). Don't bother with the entry hole at this point; you can drill it after the log siding is in place. The side walls are only 3" high, to leave a 1" ventilation space between their tops and the roof. You can get both of these from one 7"-long piece of 1 x 8 by ripping the board twice. The leftovers will prove useful later.

You'll need four 4' lengths and part of another 3' length of 3/4" dowel for the logs. Go ahead and rip all these in half on the tablesaw. The accompanying cutting chart and diagram give you the dimensions of the various logs. The specified lengths allow for final trimming to square up the ends and to miter to the correct angle. Note also that the logs on the front and back and below the roofline will overhang to be flush with the side logs.

Before siding the house, cut out the 2" x 3" door and the two 1-1/4" x 2" windows from 3/8" plywood and the 1 x 3/4" x 4" door awning from that scrap of 1 x 8 left from the side walls. Beveling the overhang to 30° or so is a nice touch. Nail and glue these parts in place at the following locations: the front door

2" from the left wall, the overhang 1-3/4" from the left wall and flush to the top of the door, and the windows 1-3/4" from an end. (We alternated ours front and back.)

Now apply the siding, butting the pieces snugly against the door, overhang, and windows. (Be careful not to put any nails where the entry hole will be.) With that done, run the walls through the tablesaw, inside down, to square up the ends of the logs. Test fit the front and back walls to the sides to get the overlap just right. Then set the miter gauge to the roof slope angle and trim all the upper logs flush with the front and back walls. At this point, you can also drill the 1-1/2" entry hole centered 2-1/2" below the roof peak.

Assemble the walls of the house with 8d galvanized finish nails; drilling lead holes here will help avoid having deviant nails emerge from the walls.

The base of the house is 1 x 8 x 7", trimmed to fit loosely between the walls. Rather than being nailed in place, it's held by four removable 3/16" x 4" bent steel rods, to offer access for cleaning. Set the house on its side with the floor in place, and bore the 3/16" holes for the rods through the side walls and into the base.

Two 11" pieces of 1 x 8, with one edge beveled to match the roof slope (about 37°), make up the roof. Nail these to the tops of the front and back walls and to the central ridge beam made from a 7" length of scrap. A bead of silicone caulk will help seal the roof's peak.

The finishing touch is the chimney, made of a piece of 1 x 2 about 2-1/2" long. For authentic stovepipe, add an inch of 1/4" dowel to the top of that.

Dark stain helps the birch dowels better resemble bark-on logs, and a coating of water sealer will prevent the wood from graying so quickly. Neighbors will be none the wiser, and your feathered friends won't say a word.

The Mountain Finch

## Log Facade Cutting Chart

| Code | Qty. | Size |
| --- | --- | --- |
| A | 4 | 2-1/2" |
| B | 4 | 5-1/4" |
| C | 1 | 2-1/4" |
| D | 1 | 3-1/2" |
| E | 7 | 9-3/4" |
| F | 2 | 7" |
| G | 2 | 5" |
| H | 2 | 3" |
| I | 2 | 1" |
| J | 2 | 8-3/4" |
| K | 6 | 2" |
| L | 6 | 5-3/4" |
| M | 2 | 1-1/4" |

WALLS STOP
BEFORE ROOF

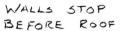

# Barn Owl Barn

## MATERIALS LIST

- (2) 1 X 10-5/8" X 20"
  Western red cedar
- (2) 1 X 8-1/2" X 20"
  Western red cedar
- (4) 1 X 8 X 22" Beveled,
  notch-lap siding
- 2 X 2 X 22-5/8" Western
  red cedar
- (2) 1/2" x 3/4" x 7" Western
  red cedar
- (3) 1/2" x 3/4" x 3-1/2"
  Western red cedar
- (4) 1/2" x 3/4" x 4" Western
  red cedar
- (10) no.8 x 1-1/4" Brass
  flathead woodscrews
- (4) Button screw hole plugs
- 8d Galvanized finish nails
- 6d Galvanized finish nails
- 4d Galvanized finish nails

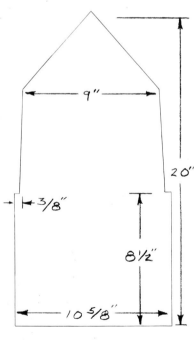

**A barn owl's nesting needs are unique, precluding this house's use by other common species. No matter. To our way of thinking, the exhilaration of discovering this silent predator overhead, faintly silhouetted against the night sky, is worth every effort to offer suitable habitat.**

Fittingly enough, the construction techniques used in the Owl Barn are unique among this collection. Nearly all its parts are from western red cedar, some of them plain boards and others of beveled, notch-lap siding. Start by cutting out the front and back walls from 1 x 12, using the accompanying cutting diagram. It's important to follow the dimensions closely, so the siding will fit snugly. Once that's done, bore the 6" hole (or cut it out with a saber or coping saw) 5" on center above the base.

Next, rip a piece of 1 x 12 that's 20-1/8" long down to 8-1/2" width. Then, cut the board exactly in half to form the two walls. To simulate barn siding, we cut 1/16"-deep saw kerfs every 1-1/4" along these boards. Countersink no.8 x 1-1/4" brass flathead woodscrews through the sides and into the edges of the front and back walls. Cover the screws with button screw hole plugs.

The roof of the house consists for four 22" pieces of 1 x 8 beveled, notch-lap siding. Overlap these boards an equal amount front and rear, and nail them to the walls with 6d galvanized finish nails. To cover the roof peak, cut a 22-5/8" piece of 2 x 2. Next, tilt the tablesaw blade to 45° and set the rip fence so it's 1/4" from the base of the blade. Run the 2 x 2 through in both directions to bevel its sides. Next, set the blade height to 1/2" and move the rip fence in so that it's 1/8" from the base of the blade. Create a W notch in the 2 x 2 by pushing it through twice. The remaining stock in the center of the notch fits into the gap between the roof boards. Miter each end of this board about 30°, and secure it to the roof peak by nailing it from the underside.

Prepare the base by ripping an 18-1/2"-long piece of 3/4" cedar down to a width of 10-5/8". Drill 1/4" drain holes in the corners and center of this floor, and secure the board with screws countersunk through the walls and into the edge of the floor.

All the decorative trim is formed from 1/2" x 3/4" stock. Prepare about 4' of this material by ripping strips from the edge of a piece of 1x cedar. To trim the entry hole to look like a barn door, set your miter gauge to 22-1/2°, and cut two 7" pieces mitered on one end and three 3-1/2" pieces mitered on both ends. For the loft, reset the miter gauge to 45°, and cut four 4" strips mitered at both ends.

Black was the unquestioned choice for coloring the roof, but we have to admit to being torn about painting the cedar walls. The red works well—perhaps counterpointed by a white billboard on the roof?—but the walls might also have been effective left natural. In any event, the white trim offers worthwhile visual relief. The decorative wagon wheel came from a shopping spree in the doll house section at a local craft store. Likewise, model railroad shops offer a variety of knickknacks that can enhance a fanciful bird house.

The Female Short-Eared Owl

# The Little House Out Back

**Here's a one-holer of a different sort. Although not as ornate (or imposing!) as some of our nest boxes, this little shelter, modeled after the standard rural backyard convenience, is both eminently practical—since it can be sized to suit many of the smaller house-nesting bird species—and loaded with enough boondocks charm to serve as an indoor conversation piece, complementing any country decor.**

Its construction is far from difficult, too. The entire house is cut from 1x pine and held together with 6d galvanized finish nails.

Begin by shaping the two sides of the roof. First cut a 1 x 6 to a length of 15-1/8" (a blade width longer than two roof sides). Then set your table saw blade to 30°, and rip one edge of the board to establish the peak bevel. Crosscut this board exactly in the middle, and you'll end up with two 1 x 6 x 7-1/2" roof boards. To support the roof peak from the under side and offer additional weather protection, cut two 30° bevels to form a 60° edge on a piece of 1x scrap about 5-3/8" long. A second length of 1x scrap, ripped to 1" thickness, can be sawn to length to form the angled perch.

Working downward, miter one end of each 1 x 4" x 10" front and back board to form the 60° peak. In one of these, bore the 1-1/4" diameter entry hole 1-3/4" on center below the peak. (You can later paint the tell-tale crescent moon in black as we've done. Or, as an alternative, use a jig-saw to cut out a moon large enough to contain the hole desired; then back that crescent with a black-painted scrap of 1/4" plywood in which the actual entry hole has been bored.) The back ought to have a 1/4" hole for mounting. The perch, which you cut in the previous paragraph, is nailed an inch below the hole at about a 30° angle.

The sides of the house are each 1 x 6 x 8-1/2", with the tops beveled at 30° to parallel the roof. Align the bases of these walls with the bases of the front and back; the gap between the top of the wall and the roof is left for ventilation.

With that done, simply cut out the oversized 1 x 6 x 7-1/2" base and the 1 x 3-15/16" x 3-15/16" base plug, which measures slightly smaller than the interior of the finished bird house. (Remember, if this fit is too snug, warpage will make the base difficult to remove for cleaning.) Nail these two parts together, centering the square in the width and positioning it 1-1/4" from the back of the base. Then drill 1/4" drainage holes.

Use a rasp and/or sandpaper to smooth any sharp corners, and assemble the bird house, securing each joint with glue and nails. Overlap the roof boards 1/2" to the rear, so the front receives the most weather protection. Then fit the base piece into the structure, and drill 1/4" holes toward the front of the right side and the rear of the left side, close enough to the bottom to allow the bit to go cleanly through the wall and into the interior base. Use a vise to bend two short pieces of 3/16" steel rod, which will hold the whole assembly together until it's time for spring cleaning.

It's our feeling that the outhouse should have a rustic look. So, other than painting the moon, you might limit your brush work to the application of a clear sealant on the rest of the structure, hoping it'll achieve a weathered look in time. Further authenticity might be added by covering the peak with a glued-on scrap of asphalt roofing paper.

Finally, mount the little house where you can keep an eye on it. Once your guests have taken up residence, you'll want to be "privy" to their comings and goings.

The Nuthatch

## MATERIALS LIST

(2) 1 x 6 x 7-1/2" Pine
(2) 1 x 4" x 10" Pine
1 x 1" x 3" Pine
(2) 1 x 6 x 8-1/2" Pine
1 x 6 x 7-1/2" Pine
1 x 3-15/16" x 3-15/16" Pine
3/16" Steel rod
6d Galvanized finish nails

## MATERIALS LIST

(2) 1 x 7-1/4" x 9" Pine
(2) 1 x 6 x 7" Pine
1 x 1" x 3" Pine
(2) 1 x 4-1/2" x 4-1/2" Pine
1 x 4-1/4" x 7-3/4" Pine
1 x 2" x 4-7/16" Pine
6d Galvanized finish nails
no.8 x 1-1/2" Brass flathead
    woodscrews

**It's amazing how a few simple changes in shape and decoration can take a bird house from the ridiculous to the sublime, transforming it from a backwoods commode into a post house at the guarded border of a mythical country.**

Most of the procedures for building this bird house are the same as those used for the outhouse, the main difference being the sloped walls. Start with the 1 x 7-1/4" x 9" roof boards, sawing them from a 1 x 8 x 18-1/8" beveled at 30°. Again, an appropriately beveled piece of 1x ought to be cut to go beneath the peak for support and weather protection.

Next, miter 60° points in two 7" lengths of 1 x 6. Find the center of the base (2-3/4" from either edge) of one, mark points 1-13/16" on both sides of the center, and connect these points with outer edges of the roof peak bevels. Now, stacking the marked piece atop the other one with their square bases against the miter gauge, set the gauge to the appropriate angle (about 10°), cut, flop, and cut again. At this time, go ahead and bore the 1-1/4" entry hole centered 2-1/2" below the peak. The 1 x 1" x 3" perch can also be formed and nailed in place.

To bevel the bottoms of the sides, start with about 10 inches of 1 x 6" pine, set the tablesaw blade to the same angle used to profile the front and back, and rip the board to leave a 4-1/2" width. Return the blade to vertical and cut out two 4-1/2" pieces from this stock.

The 1 x 4-1/4" x 7-3/4" base of the guardhouse and its 1 x 2" x 4-7/16" interior floor can now be cut, remembering that the latter is sized to allow for a little warpage. Position the floor centered in the width of the base and 1-1/4" from the back, nail the two pieces together, and drill the 1/4" drainage holes in the assembly. With that done, use 6d galvanized finish nails and glue to assemble the guardhouse. Then insert the base and drill and countersink holes to accommodate the no.8 x 1-1/2" brass flathead wood screws that will hold everything together until you need to clean it out.

The Yellow Wren

We choose a jaunty diagonally-striped paint scheme to make our guard post visible to weary travelers, but this basic bird house shape lends itself to many interpretations. For instance, with a 1" x 1" x 1" red chimney, dark roof, pastel walls and some painted-on windows, the guardhouse could be transformed into a country cottage. Whatever exterior decor you decide on, we're sure that you'll find each year's new flock of immigrants welcome additions to the population of your own backyard kingdom.

*Spare the Perch*

*The color scheme of this house may be a bit off-putting to its intended tenants, wrens. To discourage sparrows—which have considerably less discriminating taste in housing—from taking over, omit the perch from this design.*

# Sky-Way Toll-Booth

**Two-sided nesting platforms, preferred by robins and other claustrophobic species, are probably the simplest of bird houses. Still, as our toll-booth platform proves, even a basic design can come into its own with creative use of paints and accessories.**

The platform itself couldn't be much easier to make. To begin, cut three rectangles from 1x lumber. The first, 8-1/8" x 9" will form the roof; the second, 8-1/8" x 12", the back; and the third, 7" x 8-1/8", the base. Next, cut a 6" x 9-1/2" rectangle, and miter one end at 45° to form a peak. (At this time you might also want to cut the 45° wedge from one of the short ends of the roof so it will fit flush with the wall and back.) Now use a jig saw, coping saw, or band saw to cut the scoop, as shown, from the front of the single wall. The roof, wall, back and floor can be assembled now, using no.8 x 1-1/4" brass flathead woodscrews and glue, or set aside for painting prior to final assembly.

The window consists of a 2" x 3" block of 1/2" plywood. The stop sign and barrier will probably call for jig-saw work; both are cut from 1/4" plywood (or any thin stock). The coin box has several parts. First, butt two 1x blocks, one 3/4" x 2-1/2" and the other 1-1/2" x 2-1/2". The spacers, which separate the two above blocks and leave room for the toll gate, are cut from 1/4" scrap. Make the first approximately 3/4" x 1-1/4" and the second about 1/2" x 3/4". The cap is a halved length of 3/4" dowel, cut to span the top of the block and spacer assembly.

At this point you should probably paint the various components with exterior grade alkyd or latex paint. We chose bright green and yellow for the nesting platform itself, silver for the coin box, and black and yellow stripes for the toll gate. You might want to personalize your platform by taking a spin on the nearest expressway and copying the color scheme used there. (A tip: If you don't feel up to painting the details on the stop sign, check your local hobby store. They'll probably have similar signs ready-made for model railroads.)

When the finish has dried, complete the assembly, using 4d galvanized finish nails and glue to trap the gate between the coin-box blocks and to fasten the half-dowel in place. Simply glue the stop sign and window on.

All that's left is to hang your toll booth in the nearest flight path. Chances are a platform-nesting bird family will be moved to stop, and that they'll pay an ample toll in the beauty and wonder they bring to your backyard.

## MATERIALS LIST

1 x 8-1/8" x 9" Pine
1 x 8-1/8" x 12" Pine
1 x 7" x 8-1/8" Pine
1 x 6" x 9-1/2" Pine
1/2" x 2" x 3" Plywood
1 x 3/4" x 2-1/2" Pine
1 x 1-1/2" x 2-1/2" Pine
1/4" x 2" x 15" Plywood
1/4" x 3/4" x 1-1/4"
    Plywood
1/4" x 1/2" x 3/4" Plywood
3/4" Dowel
4d Galvanized finish nails

The Redbreast

# Bill Telephone

**It may not have the portability of the newest cellular phones, but we think that our rendition of "Ma Bill's" basic black unit will get a lot of use (especially during "beak" calling hours). Better still, it's fairly simply to construct (with most of the pieces fashioned from common 1x pine) and should be as appealing to birds hoping to phone home as it is to its builders.**

The sides begin as 1 x 8 x 18" rectangles. From one long edge of each, cut away a strip measuring 1-1/4" x 13-1/4". Then miter the step produced by this cut at a 15° angle, and cut a matching miter on the narrow top end.

The front of the phone is a piece of 1 x 6 measuring 15-3/4" long, while the back is a 1 x 6 x 20". Both boards should have 15° bevel cuts on one end. The roof is simply a 7-1/4" length of 1 x 8, and will later be fastened to the back with cabinet hinges. At this time you can also drill the 1-1/2" entry hole, centered 2-1/2" from the top of the front panel.

A directory shelf juts forward over the mitered step. Cut from 1 x 8, it measures 3-3/4", and one long end is beveled to 15° to mount flush with the front panel. Below it, you'll want to install a false front consisting of a 1 x 6 x 3-5/8" board.

The bird house was designed with two bases: One, a false floor, is a 1 x 6 piece measuring 5-1/2" and will be mounted flush with the bottom of the walls; the real base can be moved up inside to determine the depth of the nesting chamber. It measures the same as the false base, and ours is positioned 6" up from the bottom of the phone. Each should be drilled with four 1/2" drainage holes.

Assemble the sides and front first, using glue and 6d galvanized finish nails. Then position the bases, secure them on three sides, and go on to add the back and false front.

The dial is cut from 1/4" plywood with a 4" hole saw. An entry hole, matching that in the front of the bird house, is centered on this disc,

and a ring of 1/2" holes complete the piece, which can be glued in place.

To make the mouthpiece, use a 2-1/2" hole saw to cut a disc from a scrap of 1x, and tap nails onto its upper surface to produce a perforated texture. Mount this to a 1-1/2" x 1-1/2" x 3" base, and secure it, at a jaunty angle, to the front of the phone with a drill, glue, and a short section of 3/8" dowel.

The earpiece is simply a 2" x 4" block cut from 2x stock, then rasped and sanded to a bell-shaped flare. The top is drilled to accept the glued-in cord (either old electrical wire or heavy black nylon cord), the other end of which is knotted through a hole in the side of the phone.

Once it's painted to your liking, hang it from a likely tree. Then set a chair on the porch, pour a cold drink, take the indoor phone off the hook, and enjoy a restful evening waiting for . . . what else? Bird calls!

## MATERIALS LIST

(2) 1 x 8 x 18" Pine
1 x 6 x 15-3/4" Pine
1 x 8 x 7-1/4" Pine
1 x 8 x 3-3/4" Pine
1 x 6 x 3-5/8" Pine
1 x 6 x 5-1/2" Pine
1/4" x 4" x 4" Plywood
1-1/2" x 1-1/2" x 3" Pine
3/8" x 3" Dowel
2 x 2" x 4" Pine
Black cord

The Jay

# The Red Caboose

**Is there a train-lover in your family or circle of friends? The odds are that your answer will be "yes", because locomotives seem to weave a web of attraction that enfolds model railroaders and aficionados of the real thing alike. And the caboose, celebrated in folk songs and children's tales, has a charm that appeals even to those of us who aren't among the locomotion faithful. We offer this bird house design as an emblem of enthusiasm for train buffs that may also enchant those of us who've never felt the call of the rhythm of the rails.**

Virtually all of the pieces can be cut from 1x stock. The base (and its matching roof), for example, are 18" lengths of 1 x 8. The wheel blocks are among the few exceptions to this rule, each being a 4" section of 2 x 4. Use a hole saw to make the eight 1-1/2"-diameter wheels from scraps of 1x stock, and secure them to the blocks with no.8 x 1-1/2" brass flathead woodscrews.

Building upward, you'll need to cut two interior cab supports, each 1 x 1" x 4-1/2". These will fit inside the cab and provide a seat for the screws that hold it to the base. The sides of the cab are cut from 1 x 6, each measuring 14" long. Then, from the same 1 x 6 stock, you'll need to cut four 4-1/2" sections to serve as the ends and interior partitions.

The holes—centered 2" down from the top edge and spaced at 2-1/2", 7", and 11-1/2" intervals—are 1-1/2" in diameter. The outer two are "dummies", backed with scrap lumber and painted black to simulate openings. (We chose to block off the interior to create a single compartment of standard floor dimensions. Another alternative would be to make a three-apartment caboose for purple martins.) The partitions that create the dummy chambers are positioned 2-1/2" from each end of the cab. The perches are simply 2" pieces of 3/8" dowel, glued into 1/4"-deep 3/8" holes.

The upper cab is also cut from 1x stock. Its roof measures 7" x 7-1/2", its sides each 2-1/2" x 5-1/2", and its front and back panels each 2-1/4" x 4-1/2". (The latter are mounted flush to the roof of the main cab, leaving 1/4" vent slots along their top edges. Be sure, also, to drill four or five 3/8" vent holes in the roof beneath the upper cab, and a quartet of the same to drain the floor of the nesting compartment.)

The windows that trim both upper and lower cabs are cut from 1/4" plywood. The lower two each measure 2" x 3", those on the sides of the upper cab are each 1-1/4" x 2", and the single pane on the upper back measures 1" x 2".

The smokestack, a 2" piece of 5/8" dowel, is set into a drilled 1/4" x 1-1/2" x 3/4" base (cut from plywood). The roof trim is formed by ripping 3/4" dowel in half. The sections measure 8-3/4" and 4-1/4", each allowing a little overhang. Finally, the guard rails on the front and the rear of the base are formed from 3/16" steel rod, and pushed into pre-drilled holes.

Most of the assembly can be handled with glue and 8d galvanized finish nails (though you might prefer to paint the caboose before putting it together). The cab, however, is secured to its interior braces with easily removable no.8 x 1-1/2" brass flathead woodscrews.

We chose to paint our nest box in a sort of "generic caboose" red and black. If you'd like to get more adventurous, try to duplicate an actual caboose from a local line (or the one that brings up the rear of your personal train set).

Yes, the glory days of the rails might be behind us, but with air travel becoming less reliable and less affordable, perhaps our little red caboose will entice a few feathered frequent flyers to try something different . . . to take the train.

The Willow Wren

## MATERIALS LIST

(2) 1 x 8 x 18" Pine
(2) 2 x 4 x 4" Pine
1 x 2" x 15" Pine
(2) 1 x 1" x 4-1/2" Pine
(2) 1 x 6 x 14" Pine
(4) 1 x 6 x 4-1/2" Pine
(3) 3/8" x 2" Dowels
1 x 7" x 7-1/2" Pine
(2) 1 x 2-1/2" x 5-1/2" Pine
(2) 1 x 2-1/4" x 4-1/2" Pine
(2) 1/4" x 2" x 3" Plywood
(2) 1/4" x 1-1/4" x 2"
   Plywood
1/4" x 1 x 2 Plywood
5/8" x 2" Dowel
1/4" x 1-1/2" x 3/4"
   Plywood
3/4" x 14" Dowel
3/16" x 16" Steel rod
8d Galvanized finish nails
(2) no.8 x 1-1/2" Brass
   flathead woodscrews

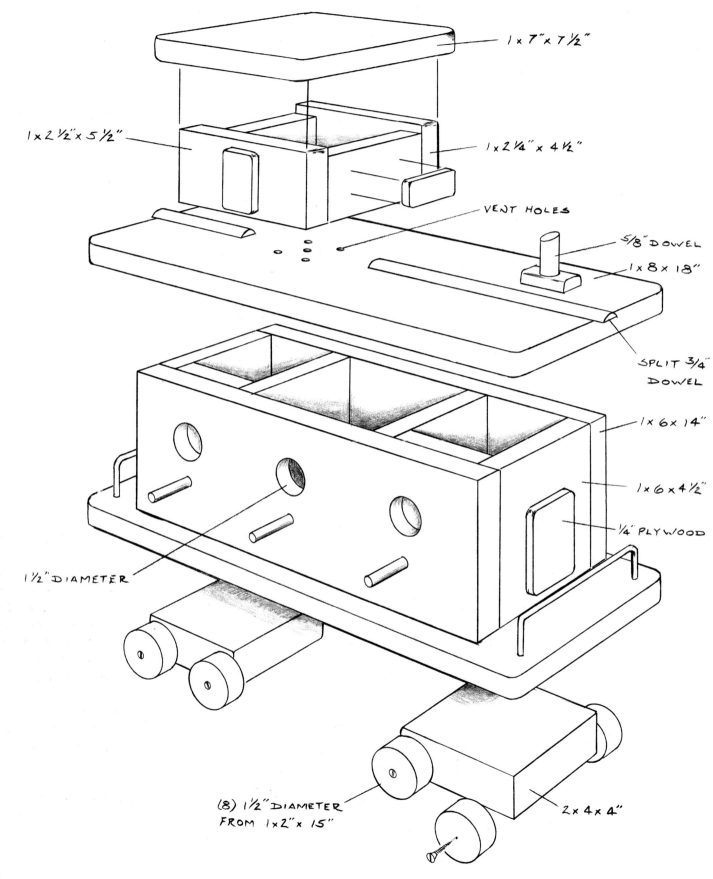

1 x 7" x 7 1/2"

1 x 2 1/2" x 5 1/2"

1 x 2 1/4" x 4 1/2"

VENT HOLES

5/8" DOWEL

1 x 8 x 18"

SPLIT 3/4" DOWEL

1 x 6 x 14"

1 x 6 x 4 1/2"

1/4" PLYWOOD

1 1/2" DIAMETER

(8) 1/2" DIAMETER
FROM 1 x 2" x 15"

2 x 4 x 4"

# Ship of Fowls

**Since Noah found land with the help of a dove, it seems appropriate that this miniature ark return the favor—by serving as a feeder or nesting platform for our feathered friends.**

All of the components of this bird boat can be cut from 1x lumber. Begin by drawing one side on a 12 x 23" board. (Either use the template provided here, or sketch a suitably nautical shape freehand.) Use a jig saw, coping saw, or band saw to cut out one side, then use that board as a pattern to trace the shape for its duplicate.

The front and rear panels of the ark, again consisting of 1x stock, are each 6" x 9-1/2", with their tops and bottoms beveled 10° so they'll be horizontal when the planks are fastened in place. The deck measures 9-1/2" x 18" and has the same 10° bevel on each of its ends to allow the flush mounting of the front and rear panels. Also, to provide adequate drainage in foul weather, five saw kerfs—each centered, 12" long, and 1-1/2" apart—should be cut into the deck.

The cabin is also fairly simple to fashion. Its two sides are 7-1/2" x 9-3/4", each with a 45° bevel at one end to meet the roof. The front and back begin as 6" x 12-5/8" planks, which are then mitered to form the 90° peaks. Now, on each of these four panels, measure 5-1/2" up from the bottom and use that point to center a 4" hole saw. Bore the hole, and then run straight cuts from the holes' outer edges to complete the arches.

Finally, the roof consists of two 7" x 10" panels, each beveled 45° on its 10" sides. The ark can be painted either before or after assembling it with no. 8 x 1-1/2" brass flathead wood screws. Then, once you've decked the deck with a selection of plastic or wooden toy animals, you're ready to invite the birds to come…two by two.

## MATERIALS LIST

1 x 12 x 23" Pine
(2) 1 x 6" x 9-1/2" Pine
1 x 9-1/2" x 18" Pine
(2) 1 x 7-1/2" x 9-3/4" Pine
(2) 1 x 6" x 12-5/8" Pine
(2) 1 x 7" x 10" Pine
(20) no.8 x 1-1/2" Brass flathead woodscrews

The Turtle Dove

*Broad Boards*

*A few of the houses in this book use 1 x 12 lumber in their construction. These days it's not easy to find a quality board that wide, since old-growth forests are mostly gone, and second- and third-growth trees are harvested at a comparatively young age. If you can't locate kiln-dried, unwarped 1 x 12s, consider substituting plywood in this and other designs.*

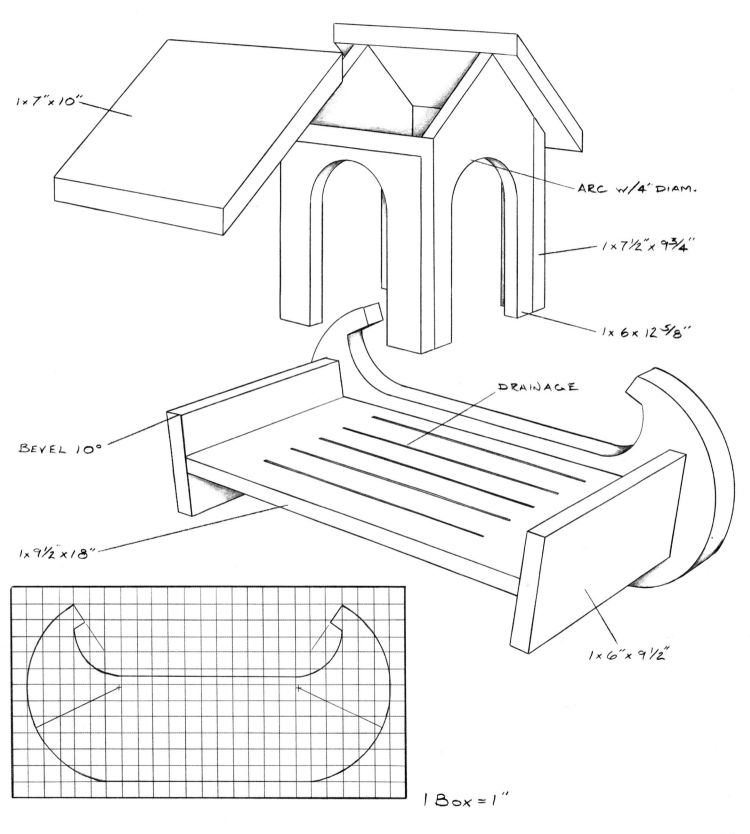

1 x 7" x 10"

ARC w/4" DIAM.

1 x 7½" x 9¾"

1 x 6 x 12⅝"

DRAINAGE

BEVEL 10°

1 x 9½" x 18"

1 x 6" x 9½"

1 Box = 1"

# The Skyrocket

**You can celebrate with fireworks year around with this bird house, which perches atop its mounting pole as if waiting for an oversized match. And, though you'll get no star bursts from our rocket, we're betting that any bird with a sense of adventure will get a bang out of it!**

## MATERIALS LIST

(2) 1 x 8 x 26" Pine
(2) 1 x 6 x 22-1/2" Pine
(2) 1 x 8 x 8-1/2 Pine
1 x 4 x 32" Pine
1 x 2-3/4" x 5-1/4" Pine
(3) 1 x 3/4" x 2" Pine
1 x 5-3/8" x 5-5/8" Pine
(8) no.8 x 1-1/2" Brass
flathead woodscrews
6d Galvanized finish nails
3/16" x 12" Steel rod

To begin, cut two 26" lengths of 1 x 8, and double miter one end of each to produce a 60° peak. Then designate one as the front of the rocket and, at a point 15" from the peak, cut it in two on a 45° bevel angling away from the peak. The two sides, cut from 1 x 6, measure 22-1/2" long. The roof can also be cut from 1 x 8 stock. Each side is 8-1/2" long, with a 30° bevel on its long edge.

You'll need a 32" length of 1 x 4 to make the fins. First draw a perpendicular line across the center, and then divide each of the two rectangles thus formed with another line, creating four right triangles. Measure 3" up from the 90° corner of each of these, and draw a line to angle across the 4" dimension to the larger acute corner. Finally, measure 3" down from the smaller acute angle of each, and draw a perpendicular line intersecting the hypotenuse. Now simply cut out the four fins thus drawn.

The Green Woodpecker

You'll need to turn to 1x scrap for the rest of the components. The awning that will cover the entry hole (which should be 1-1/2" in diameter and centered 7-1/2" below the peak) measures 2-3/4" x 5-1/4", with a 30° bevel on one long edge. It is supported by two 3/4" x 2" braces, each beveled to 30° at one end to meet the awning. The perch measures 3/4" x 2". And finally, the floor—which will be positioned 8-1/2" from the base of the rocket, and which should incorporate four evenly spaced 1/2" drainage holes—measures about 5-3/8" x 5-5/8". (This may be a loose fit, which is perfectly alright as it'll offer additional ventilation and drainage.)

Begin the assembly process by attaching the fins to the sides, from inside, with no.8 x 1-1/2" brass flathead wood screws. Then join the sides to the back with 6d galvanized finish nails. (Leave the gap at the top, as this will provide ventilation.) With that done, secure the floor on three sides, and then go on to fasten the upper front panel, the roof, the awning, and the perch in place with 6d galvanized finish nails.

Now slip the lower front panel into position, and drill three 3/16" holes, each 2-3/4" deep, through the panel and into the sides. Two of these should be on one side, the third on the other. Three 3-1/4" lengths of 3/16" steel rod, each with a 90 degree angle formed 3/4" from one end, can be pushed through these holes, securing the lower front while allowing easy access to the birdhouse's interior.

As you can see from our example, the rocket's paint scheme should provide a good opportunity to let your imagination run wild. We got our inspiration from roadside fireworks stands. You might take a similar approach, or simply coat the whole nest box in a "firecracker" red. Then again, you could choose more muted colors, in deference to the less adventurous birds that might thus be tempted to take up residence.

It's up to you. After all, the sky's the limit!

# Dutch Treat

As you've certainly discovered by now, we firmly maintain that nest boxes should serve people as well as birds. Take the windmill pictured here, for example. While it could certainly offer a welcoming rental to would-be avian parents, it would also make a striking centerpiece for a flower garden (anyone for tulips?), function as a unique front-yard whirligig, or add a little old-world charm to an interior decor.

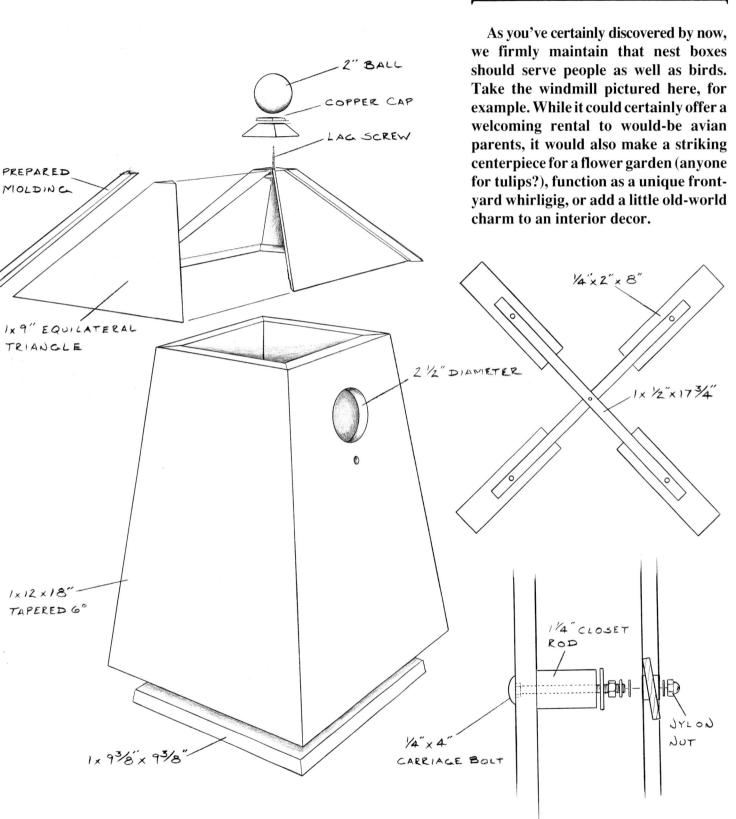

2" BALL

COPPER CAP

LAG SCREW

PREPARED MOLDING

1 x 9" EQUILATERAL TRIANGLE

2 ½" DIAMETER

1 x 12 x 18" TAPERED 6°

1 x 9⅜" x 9⅜"

¼" x 2" x 8"

1 x ½" x 17¾"

1¼" CLOSET ROD

¼" x 4" CARRIAGE BOLT

NYLON NUT

**But you seldom get something for nothing, and the pleasingly simply lines of this birdhouse belie some fairly intricate construction steps.**

The house itself isn't too imposing, however, and can all be cut from 1x lumber. Each side begins as a 1 x 12 x 18" board. The long edges are then ripped at a taper of about 6° to form a 7-1/2" x 11-1/4" x 18" trapezoid, with all long sides beveled to 45°. The mitered corners of the box can then be assembled with cabinet-maker's corner fasteners in the end grain at each open end. The base will measure 9-3/8" square, incorporate a 1/2" drainage hole near each corner, and have each side beveled to 6° to allow it to be slipped up into the larger end of the box. It should be secured with no.8 x 1-1/2" brass flathead wood screws, allowing its removal for cleaning. The hole (which we've put behind the blades for our photograph, but which you might want to place on the back of the house if you hope to attract birds) is centered 4-1/2" from the top, and is 2-1/2" in diameter.

The roof consists of four 9" equilateral triangles, each beveled to 45° on two of its adjoining sides. Come down 1-1/2" from each beveled peak, and cut off the point with your saw blade set at 45° to form a level platform for the peak ornament when the panels are assembled. To give the roof a seat on the base, dado a 1/4" deep, 5/8" step on the inside base of each roof panel. The roof probably won't require any further fastening, though you could glue it in place.

The roof ridges are capped with 1" x 1" x 7-7/8" trim, notched to conform to the ridges and beveled parallel at 45° at each end. It's easiest to start with a 32" length of 1" x 1" stock, cut the V-notch once, and then trim the strips to length. To cut the groove, set the blade angle to 45° and the height to 3/8", with the blade tip 1/2" from the rip fence. Run the stock through from one direction, flop it, and repeat to complete the notch.

The peak assembly consists of a 1/4" x 2-1/2" lag screw and fender washer; a 2-3/4" square 1x cap, beveled to 45° on all sides; a 2"-diameter wooden cabinet knob; and a 2" square of copper flashing. Once the roof is assembled with glue and/or 6d galvanized finish nails, the peak can be installed as shown in the illustration. (Be careful not to over tighten the knob on the lag screw, as the pressure on the washer will tend to pull apart the roof at its peak.)

The propeller axle assembly consists of a 1/4" x 4" carriage bolt, a 2" length of closet rod with a 5/16" hole drilled through its center (use a drill press if you have one), one 1/4" nylon nut, two 1/4" nylon washers, one 1/4" nylon cap nut . . . and, of course, the blades.

And what's a windmill without its sails? The blade arms measure 1 x 1/2" x 17-3/4", and are made by ripping 1/2" off a length of 1x stock. To cut the notches to accept the blades, simply set your saw blade to 10° and make 5-1/4" cuts, centered on the 1/2" dimension, into the ends of the crosspieces. Now cut 3/4" dados, 1/4" deep, centered on each arm (keep the angle on the airfoils in mind when planning these cuts), and glue the arms together before drilling a 1/4" axle hole at their center. The blades are simply 1/4" x 2" x 8" strips of lattice, fastened with glue and, if you feel the need for more security, one or two 3/16" copper rivets apiece.

Your plans for the windmill will likely influence its paint scheme. If it's to decorate a yard, flower bed, or living room, make it as bright and as intricate as your patience and abilities allow. If you hope to attract residents, however, you'd be better served by muted tones and might even want to leave it to weather naturally. Should you take the latter approach, however, do position the entry hole in the back of the house, or lock the blades in a stationary position, lest your would-be tenants risk becoming grist for your mill!

## MATERIALS LIST

(4) 1 x 12 x 18" Pine
1 x 9-3/8" x 9-3/8" Pine
(4) no.8 x 1-1/2 Brass
    flathead woodscrews
(4) 1 x 9" x 9" Pine
(4) 1" x 1" x 7-7/8" Pine
1/4" x 2-1/2" Lag screw
1/4" Fender washer
1 x 2-3/4" x 2-3/4" Pine
2" Cabinet knob
2" x 2" Copper flashing
6d Galvanized finish nails
1/4" x 4" Carriage bolt
2" Closet rod
(2) 1/4" Nylon wawshers
1/4" Nylon nut
1/4" Nylon cap nut
(2) 1 x 1/2" x 17-3/4" Pine
(4) 1/4" x 2" x 8" Lattice
(8) 3/16" Copper rivets

# A Tudor Coop

To our way of thinking, there are few more homey looking house designs than the classic Tudor cottage. This nest box is an attempt to translate that warm charm in miniature—to create a bird house that's as appealing as it is practical, and that's subtle enough in color and trim to attract the most timid of species.

*If you'd like to take this house one step further, adding real thatch is the logical choice. Consider weaving together sprigs of dried grasses, or, for a ready solution, sacrifice a whisk broom to your Tudor's roof.*

The Black-Headed Bunting

91

## MATERIALS LIST

3/4" x 8-1/4" x 8-1/4" OSB
3/4" x 7-3/4" x 8-1/4" OSB
3/4" x 2-1/2" x 8-1/4" OSB
3/4" x 1-3/4" x 8-1/4" OSB
1/2" x 6" x 11" Plywood
(2) 1/2" x 6" x 6-1/2"
  Plywood
1/2" x 4" x 6" Plywood
1 x 5" x 2" Pine
1/2" x 5" x 7-1/2" Plywood
(2) 3/4" Outside corner
  molding, 4" long
(2) 3/4" Outside corner
  molding, 2-3/4" long
(2) 3/4" Outside corner
  molding, 6-3/4" long
1 x 1/4" x 48" Pine
1/4" x 3" x 3" Plywood
3/4" x 5" x 5" Plywood
(4) no.8 x 1-1/4" Brass
flathead woodscrews
6d Galvanized finish nails

The cottage's roof is built from 3/4" oriented strand board (commonly called OSB), which provides an easy and effective means of suggesting the Tudor thatched roof. One side measures 8-1/4" x 8-1/4", and has a 60° bevel on one edge. The other is a 7-3/4" x 8-1/4" rectangle, with the 60° bevel on one long side. When they're assembled, the bevel of the shorter piece is simply butted against the face of the longer, with the bevel on the larger panel extending the slope of the former and completing the peak.

The roof cap is formed in the same manner, and consists of one 2-1/2" x 8-1/4" strip of OSB and a second strip measuring 1-3/4" x 8-1/4". All of the exposed edges of the roof pieces should be rounded on a sander to give the appearance of thatch.

The back wall (and all the other structural walls) is cut from 1/2" plywood. It begins as a 6" x 11" panel, with a double miter cut at the top to create the 60° peak. Each side wall measures 6" x 6-1/2", with a 30° bevel cut at the top. To produce the cantilever (for the overhanging "second floor"), simply cut a 1-1/2" x 4-3/4" notch from one of the 6" sides of each panel.

The "first floor" front wall measures 4" x 6", and is topped with a 1 x 5" x 2" sill, positioned across the top and extending forward enough to allow the gable wall to be secured to it while sliding between the side walls. The latter piece, again cut from 1/2" plywood, is 5" x 7-1/2", with a 60° peak mitered on one short end. (Give extra care to these cuts, as the slope of the gable wall must meet that of the bevel on the side walls, with only 3/4" corner molding to cover errors.)

All of the house's corners are trimmed with 3/4" outside corner molding. The lower front wall needs two 4" sections; the upper front will require two 2-3/4" lengths, each mitered to 30° at one end to meet the slope of the roof; and the rear will take two 6-3/4" strips with 30° miters at their upper ends.

The rest of the cottage's trim is formed by ripping 1/4" strips from 1x stock, then cutting these to fit. Use the illustration as a key; all of the angles will be either 45°, 60° or 90°.

The hole, positioned 5-1/2" on center from the peak of the second-story front, measures 1-1/2" in diameter. It receives its own piece of trim, cut from 1/4" plywood. To make this piece, first cut a disk with a 2-1/2" hole saw, then switch to a 1-1/2" hole saw, using the same pilot hole.

The base of the bird house should be cut from 3/4" plywood, and measures 5" x 5", with a quartet of 1/2" drainage holes, one near each corner. It'll be installed last, and can be secured in place with no.8 x 1-1/4" brass flathead wood screws, allowing its removal for cleaning.

Considering the complexity of the trim, you'll probably want to first check the fit of all pieces, then paint or stain them dark before final assembly. Leave the roof natural, and choose earthy colors with good contrast for the walls and trim. Be sure, as always, to use good exterior-grade paints if the house will actually be used to attract birds.

Once the pieces have dried, assemble them with glue, using 6d galvanized finish nails where required for strength.

After you've built your first Tudor bird house, you may be tempted to assemble more, perhaps even to market a few at a local crafts outlet. If so, more power to you; there's many a big business that started out as a "cottage" industry!

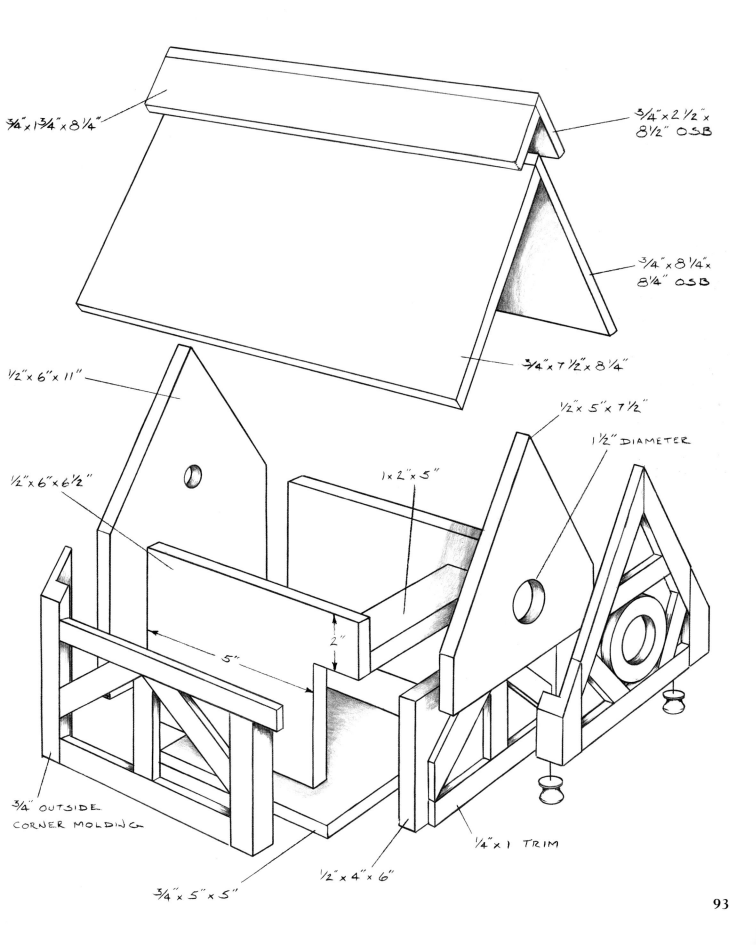

3/4" x 1 3/4" x 8 1/4"

3/4" x 2 1/2" x
8 1/2" OSB

3/4" x 8 1/4" x
8 1/4" OSB

3/4" x 7 1/2" x 8 1/4"

1/2" x 6" x 11"

1/2" x 5" x 7 1/2"

1 1/2" DIAMETER

1/2" x 6" x 6 1/2"

1 x 2" x 5"

2"

5"

3/4" OUTSIDE
CORNER MOLDING

1/4" x 1 TRIM

3/4" x 5" x 5"

1/2" x 4" x 6"

# The Cuckoo Condo

**Talk about life imitating art imitating life. The original Black Forest cuckoo clock could easily be said to mimic bird houses, with the nesting cuckoo emerging from its chamber to sing the changes of the hours, while our nest box places a family of wrens in a wooden cuckoo's role, if only to mark the changing of the seasons.**

The basic bird house, to which the decorative front face and trim will be attached, is cut from 1/2" plywood. Each half of the roof consists of a 7" x 8" rectangle, with one of its long sides mitered at 45° to form half of the right-angled peak. Each side panel is a simple 6" x 6-1/2" block. (These are not mitered and will be mounted flush with the base in order to leave ventilation slots under the roof.) The front and back walls begin as 5" x 10-1/2" rectangles, then are mitered to form a 90° point.

The false front begins as a 9-1/4" x 15-3/4" piece of 3/4" ply. Use your miter gauge to cut a 90° peak on one end, then draw a line across the base of that triangle, find its center, and mark points 3" from each side of it. Line up those points with their respective lower corners, and scribe two lines, each stretching the full length of the board, to mark the sloping sides. Then cut along these lines.

Now mark the center point of the base and, positioning a 4"-diameter can lid in such a way that it's centered and just touching the mark, trace the hemisphere that will form the bottom of the decorative scroll. Place the same jar lid on one side of the hemisphere, so that 1/4 of its arc swings from the upper edge of the half circle to the side of the panel, and trace that arc. Do the same on the far side. Use a jig saw, coping saw, or band saw to cut along the lines, being careful to cut into the two sharp angles (where the curves meet) from one side before backing out the blade and completing the cut from the other direction. (You'll probably need to clean up these cuts later with a file or sandpaper.)

The two trim pieces that hang beneath the roof are cut from 3" x 6-1/2" pieces of 1/2" plywood. Miter one end of each to 45°, then trace your pattern on one, cut it out, and use the finished piece as a template for the other side. The peak cap is made from two 8"-long pieces of joint (or seam) molding ripped at 45°. Set the rip fence so that the blade will just remove one of the two smaller bumps.

Assemble the components as shown, using glue and 6d galvanized finish nails. (You might want to use no.8 x 1-1/4" brass flathead wood screws to secure the base so it can be removed for cleaning.) Go on to drill one 1/2" drainage hole near each corner of the base, and bore the 1-1/2" entry hole through both the false front and the front wall.

Now paint the clock to your liking. It could be colored a rich, chocolate brown with bright Tyrolean floral scroll work for decoration, or you could do as we did and simply treat all of the pieces with a rich, dark stain for a more natural, and traditional, look. Finally, cut a short section of stout spring, bore a small hole to accept a straightened length of one end of it, and glue the spring in place. The perch is simply a paddle of 1/2" plywood, shaped in such a way that its smaller end can be "screwed" into the coil. Stain or paint it to match the rest of the bird house.

The clock's face can be painted on as ours is. However, should you feel unequal to attempting the numerals, simply salvage an old alarm clock from a secondhand shop and cannibalize it's face and hands.

And, in no time at all, you're done. Hang it up. We think you'll soon discover that a wren in your own backyard beats a cuckoo in the Black Forest . . . (ahem) hands down.

The Cuckoo

## MATERIALS LIST

(2) 1/2" x 7" x 8" Plywood
(2) 1/2" x 6" x 6-1/2"
  Plywood
(2) 1/2" x 5" x 10-1/2"
  Plywood
3/4" x 9-1/4" x 15-3/4"
  Plywood
(2) 1/2" x 3" x 6-1/2"
  Plywood
(4) no.8 x 1-1/4" Brass
  flathead woodscrews
Steel coil spring
1/2" Plywood scrap

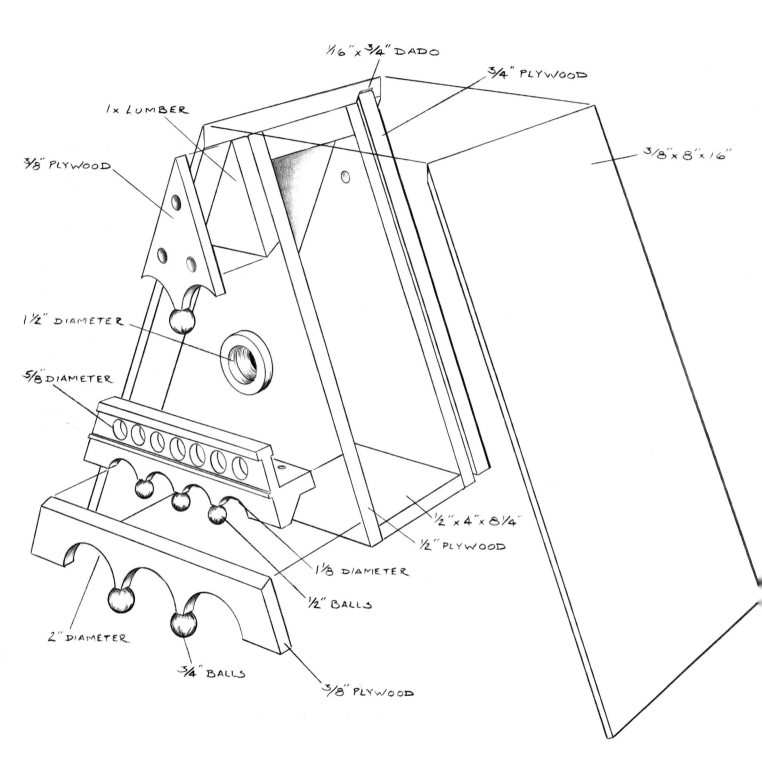

½6" x ¾" DADO

1x LUMBER

¾" PLYWOOD

3/8" PLYWOOD

3/8" x 8" x 16"

1½" DIAMETER

5/8" DIAMETER

½" x 4" x 8¼"

½" PLYWOOD

1⅛ DIAMETER

½" BALLS

2" DIAMETER

¾" BALLS

3/8" PLYWOOD

# A-Frame Chalet

**So ornate, you can almost smell the gingerbread .... If you enjoy detail work, you'll have a field day with this chalet. What our builder has done here is essentially to turn blocks of wood into sculpture using powertools.**

The frame of the house is simple enough to construct. Two 8" x 16" sections of 3/8" plywood make up the roof, and a triangle of 3/4" plywood set in a 1/16"-deep dado groove supports them.

Cutting the bevel in the roof panels at the peak does require a special technique on most tablesaws. To achieve the 19° bevel, the panels must be run through the tablesaw vertically, sliding against the rip fence. However, the point emerging from the back of the blade will be prone to drop into the blade slot, causing a dangerous jam. To avoid this, slide the plywood through on top of a sacrificial board. (You'll have to put a spacer between the plywood and the fence.)

Once you've beveled the peak, run the other ends through the saw with the boards lying flat (long side up) and the blade set at the same angle. Now adjust your dado for 3/4" width and 1/16" depth, and groove the inside of each roof panel 1/2" from the back.

The back of the roof assembly is a 38° isosceles triangle with an 8-1/4" base. Cut this board from 3/4" plywood, and glue it into the dados in the 3/8" roof panels, gluing the peak at the same time.

Now prepare two 1/2"-plywood triangles of the same dimensions as the 3/4" back. In one of them, drill the 1-1/2" entry hole 8" below the peak. To increase the depth of the entry hole, use hole saws to make a 1-1/2" x 2-1/4" ring from 3/8" plywood, and glue it over the entry hole. The two 1/2" triangles overlap a 1/2" x 4" x 8-1/4" plywood base, which has 19° bevels on each of its 4" sides. Assemble these boards, adding a 4" scrap of 1x stock near the peak for support. This main unit slides up into the roof and is held in place by a screw through each roof panel and into the base.

All the trim is permanently attached to the 1/2"-plywood main unit. Starting from the top, cut out a 38° triangle with a 2-1/4" base from 1x stock. Bevel the 2-1/4" side 45° so it won't show. The detail elements are all rendered on a 3/8" plywood triangle with a base of 4". The two arcs at the bottom are made with a 1-1/2" hole saw, and the three blue dots are just shallow holes made with a 3/8" rotary rasp. The 3/4" descending ball (from a craft store) is attached to the plywood triangle with 3/16" dowel.

Believe it or not, with the exception of the 1/2" balls, the entire porch railing started as a piece of 2 x 2-1/2" stock. A combination of tablesaw cuts and dados, along with holes and arcs bored with 5/8" and 1-1/8" bits, rendered this remarkable transformation. The profile drawing should help you work out a facsimile of the piece you see in the photo.

The lower trim piece is 3/8" plywood, 1-3/4" high bored with a 2" bit. The two balls are 3/4", and the button screw hole plugs cover two no.6 x 1" woodscrews that anchor the trim to the main unit.

Slide the finished main unit up into the roof, and countersink a no. 6 hole through each roof panel and into 1/2" plywood base of the main unit. A pair of no.6 x 1" screws hold the assembly solidly together, while leaving it easy to open for cleaning.

No other house in this collection offers such an open invitation to fancy when it comes to painting. Our painter definitely got into the spirit of it, and we imagine you will too.

## MATERIALS LIST

(2) 3/8" x 8" x 16" Plywood
3/4" x 8-1/4" x 12" Plywood
(2) 3/8" x 8-1/4" x 12" Plywood
3/8" x 2" x 2" Plywood
3/8" x 4" x 8-1/4" Plywood
1 x 2-1/4" x 3" Pine
3/8" x 4" x 5-1/2" Plywood
2 x 2-1/2" x 7" Pine
3/8" x 1-3/4" x 9" Plywood
(3) 3/4" Wooden balls
(3) 1/2" Wooden balls
(2) Button screw hole plugs
(4) no. 6 x 1" Brass flathead woodscrews

The Barred Woodpecker

# Pancho's Villa

When we were building the bird houses that make up this book, friends frequently dropped by the shop to check on our progress. Almost without exception, their attention quickly focused upon this little hacienda. And that was both surprising and gratifying, because our adobe abode is among the simplest designs we've attempted.

To begin, cut two 2'-lengths of 2 x 8, and edge-glue and clamp them to form the base. When the assembly is dry, cut off one section 9-1/2" long for the roof, leaving 14-3/8" for the base. Next, rip the 9-1/2" section of doubled 2 x 8 down to a width of 11". The front and back walls are simply 8"-long pieces cut from 2 x 8 lumber, with the entry hole—sized and positioned to suit a particular bird species—drilled

The Sand Martin

## LIST OF MATERIALS

(2) 2 x 8 x 9-1/2" Pine
(2) 2 x 8 x 14-3/8" Pine
(2) 2 x 8 x 11" Pine
(2) 2 x 8 x 8" Pine
(5) 1-1/4"-long 5/8"
    Dowels
(2) 8-1/4"-long 3/4"
    Dowels
(1) 1 x 2" x 8" Mahogany
(2) 1 x 1" x 3-1/4"
    Mahogany
(2) No. 12 x 2-1/2" Brass
    flathead woodscrews
8d Galvanized finish nails
Brick-facade adhesive

in one of them with the appropriate hole saw.

We decided to shape the side walls and roof on a tablesaw to give the house the free-form feel of adobe. You might want to eliminate this step, or simply round the corners and roof edges with a rasp or belt sander. Either way, cut an 11"-length of 2 x 8 for each wall. Then, if you choose to go our route, you'll want to taper each wall to 1" on a tablesaw. You'll have to cut the taper in from each side, then break off the trimmed section and sand any roughness from the broken joint, since the saw cuts won't quite meet in the center. Then, taper the 11"-long sides of the roof board, again using the table saw, to match the slope of the side walls.

With that done, select a 5/8" drill bit and bore five holes about 1/2" deep on the front edge of the roof to accommodate the dowel "vigas" that protrude from the eave, and two more 3/4" in diameter in the base—each centered 4" from the front edge, and 5" from a side—to accept the dowel pillars.

Now assemble the front and side walls and the roof of the structure with glue and nails, recessing the front wall about 2" underneath the eaves. Then insert scraps of dowel into the

holes to prevent their getting plugged up while using a wide putty knife to "texture" the surface of the villa with brick-facade adhesive. Leave the back wall off, but coat one side of it with adhesive, too. It'll later be slipped into the space and secured with two No. 12 x 2-1/2" brass flathead woodscrews from below to allow its removal for cleaning.

There are a number of ways to go from here. You might, for example, simply let the adhesive dry as it is, or dust the house while it's wet with fine sand, or wait until it's thoroughly dried and paint the villa with a suitable earth-toned exterior paint. The base should be treated with the same material and painted tan or an earthy red to suggest the sun-baked Southwestern desert soil.

Then stain five 5/8"-diameter x 1-1/4"-long dowels and glue them into the holes in the roof. The pillars consist of 3/4"-diameter x 8-1/4"-long dowels. Each fits into an assembly built up from 1x stock. We happened to have some mahogany scraps in the shop, which we cut down to 2" wide x 8" long for the lintel, and to 1" wide x 3-1/4" long, each end cut at a 45° angle, for the twin corbels. These have 3/4" holes about 1/2" deep to accept the pillars. Finally, it's time to landscape the yard with a plastic cactus (you'll probably be able to find one in a toy department or hobby shop.)

And that's that. It's easy to add a touch of the great Southwest to your backyard. It'll provide a *fiesta* for your eyes, and a *siesta* for weary warblers.

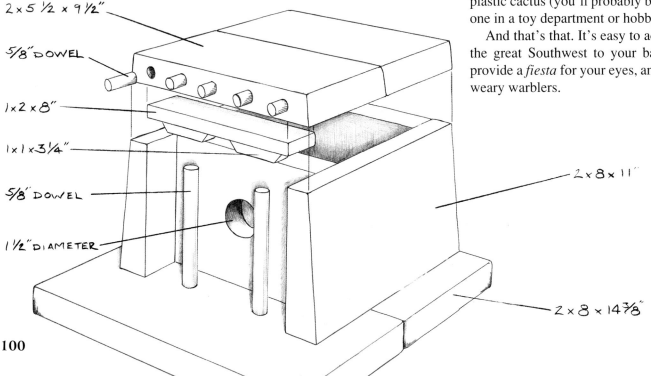

2 x 5 1/2 x 9 1/2"
5/8" DOWEL
1 x 2 x 8"
1 x 1 x 3 1/4"
5/8" DOWEL
1 1/2" DIAMETER
2 x 8 x 11"
2 x 8 x 14 3/8"

# The Cupola

While our purple-martin penthouse is unquestionably the most ambitious project in this book, it also vies for top awards in drama and practicality. Worthy in its own regard as architectural ornamentation, it offers martins a cozy but well-ventilated nesting shelter far from terrestrial hazards. And, lest you be intimidated, consider that for the most part the techniques used to build the cupola are no more involved than those used on other houses in this book. It's just bigger!

Construction of the cupola can conveniently be divided into the roof assembly and the body of the house itself. So, starting from the bottom, let's rev up the tablesaw.

**Base:** The base of the cupola is a 21"-square box made of 3/4" plywood sides that are mitered together. Two sides are rectangular, while the other two have Vs cut to match the pitch of the roof the bird house is to be mounted on. Our example is for a 12-in-12 (or 45°) roof, but you'll need to adjust to suit your own case.

Bore the 2-1/2" entry holes before assembling the house. The rectangular sides get one hole up (centered left-right and 6-1/2" below the upper edge) and three down (centered 3-3/4", 10-1/2" and 17-1/4" from a side and 13-1/4" below the upper edge). This pattern reverses on the notched sides, with the trio of holes above. Once the holes are drilled, use glue and cabinetmaker's (or chevron) plywood corner fasteners to assemble the box. To provide for mounting, cut two 19-1/2" lengths of 2 x 4 and nail them into the V so that the broad face is flush with the edge. Drill a pair of 3/8" holes 18" apart in each board to accept lag screws.

Since this is a two-story residence, you'll need two 19-1/2"-square 3/4" plywood floors. Bore a 4" hole in the center of each floor to form the central ventilation shaft. To form the 6"-square apartments, cut out eight sections of 3/4" plywood 7-1/2" high and 19-1/2" long.

These will be lapped, as in egg-crate construction, by centering 3-3/4"-deep, 3/4"-wide mortises 6-3/8" from each end. The joints should fit tightly enough that no glue or fasteners are necessary. Before assembling the partitions, drill three or four 1/2" holes toward the top of the center 6" section of each board, so each compartment can ventilate into the central shaft.

The floors should rest, unfastened, on a ledge made of 3/4" x 3/4" stock, so they can be removed for installation and later for cleaning. Position the upper surface of the bottom floor 15-3/4" above the top of the base. The second story will rest on the first-floor partitions.

The trim on the lower section is much less complicated than it first looks. There are two mitered bands of joint molding (sometimes called seam molding) located 8-7/8" and 15-3/4" from the top. And wrapping around the top is a mitered band of 1 x 4 stock with a bevel on its lower edge, and two 1/8"-deep saw kerfs 1/2" and 1" up from the bevel.

**Roof:** Use 3/4" plywood to form the 28"-square base of the roof pyramid. When you cut this piece, set the saw blade to 22° to match the roof slope. Drill five or six 1" holes in the center of this board to allow the ventilation shaft to connect with the roof.

Each roof panel is a 3/8"-plywood 68° isosceles triangle that measures 28" on the base and has a 35" height. The tip is cut off parallel to the base at a point 32-1/2" up, to leave a 2" side. (Since the joints between these panels are covered by trim, we didn't bother to bevel the edges. Should you decide to do so, be sure to add 3/4" to the width.)

The four panels come together at the top on a square of 2x stock that's tapered to 68° (to match the roof slope) and measures 2" x 2" on its smaller end. Atop that assembly goes a square of 2 x 6 x 5-1/2", beveled 1/2" at 45° top and bottom, with an inch nipped off each point and decorative 1/8"-deep saw kerfs on its vertical faces. Nail the larger piece onto the pyramid, and drill a 1-1/4" hole through the center of it and the tapered 2" x 2" square.

## MATERIALS LIST

(4) 3/4" x 21" x 30" Plywood
(2) 2 x 4 x 19-1/2" Pine
(8) 1 x 3/4" x 19-1/2" Pine
(2) 3/4" x 19-1/2" x 19-1/2" Plywood
(8) 3/4" x 7-1/2" x 19-1/2" Plywood
(8) 22-9/16"-long Joint molding
(4) 1 x 4 x 22-91/6" Pine
3/4" x 28" x 28" Plywood
(4) 28"-base, 68°, 3/8" Plywood isosceles triangles
2 x 3-7/32" x 3-7/32" Pine
2 x 6 x 5-1/2" Pine
(4) 2 x 3-3/4" x 3-3/4" Pine
(4) 2" Eave vent screens
2x Scrap Pine
12" x 12" 20 ga. Copper sheet
(4) 2 x 2" x 34" Pine
(2) 2 x 2 x 28" Pine
(8) 1-1/6" x 28" Quarter round
Drip edge
Roll roofing
Cabinetmaker's (or chevron) corner fasteners
6d Galvanized finish nails
8d Galvanized finish nails
Copper brads
(4) 3/8" x 3" Lag screws

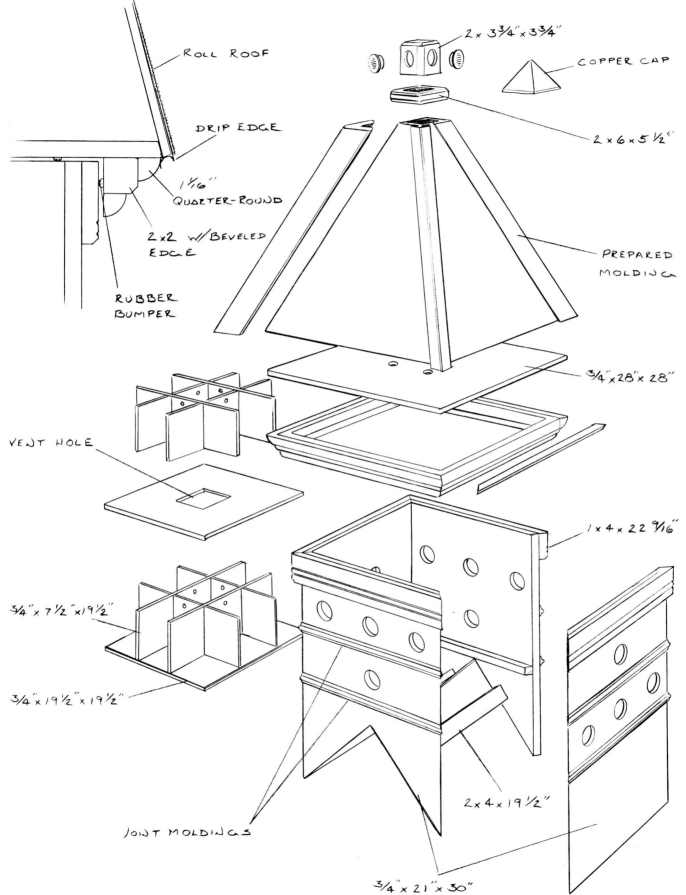

ROLL ROOF

$2 \times 3\frac{3}{4}'' \times 3\frac{3}{4}''$

COPPER CAP

DRIP EDGE

$2 \times 6 \times 5\frac{1}{2}''$

$1\frac{1}{16}''$
QUARTER-ROUND

$2 \times 2$ W/ BEVELED
EDGE

PREPARED
MOLDING

RUBBER
BUMPER

$\frac{3}{4}'' \times 28'' \times 28''$

VENT HOLE

$1 \times 4 \times 22\frac{9}{16}''$

$\frac{3}{4}'' \times 7\frac{1}{2}'' \times 19\frac{1}{2}''$

$\frac{3}{4}'' \times 19\frac{1}{2}'' \times 19\frac{1}{2}''$

$2 \times 4 \times 19\frac{1}{2}''$

JOINT MOLDINGS

$\frac{3}{4}'' \times 21'' \times 30''$

103

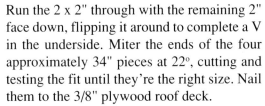

More mitered 2x makes up the cupola's cupola. You'll need to cut four pieces 3-3/4" square. Then saw dual 45° bevels on two parallel sides and a full 45° on the top of each one. In the center of each piece, bore a 2" hole, and press in an eave vent (available from any lumberyard). Now nail the parts together and use the assembly as a template to mark the location of its inside on the 2x below. Nail and glue small triangles of scrap to serve as nailers at the inside corners of this square, and complete the installation. Top the whole thing with a copper sheet-metal pyramid tacked in place with copper nails.

Roof trim consists of about 12' of 2 x 2" stock with multiple bevels. Start by setting the tablesaw blade to a 15° tilt, and then position the rip fence 1-11/16" from the base of the blade. Lay the 2 X 2" on the table with a 2" face down and run it through. Flip the board around and repeat the process. Now change the blade tilt to 45°, set the height to 3/8", and position the rip fence 1/2" from the base of the blade.

Run the 2 x 2" through with the remaining 2" face down, flipping it around to complete a V in the underside. Miter the ends of the four approximately 34" pieces at 22°, cutting and testing the fit until they're the right size. Nail them to the 3/8" plywood roof deck.

Trim under the eaves is, once again, deceptively simple. Just take 2 x 2 and cut a 1/2", 45° bevel on the lower, outside edge. Complement this with sections of 1-1/16" quarter round above and beneath the 2 x 2 stock.

We chose roll roofing for our cupola, but you'll probably want to use the same material that's on your home's roof. In any event, install "drip edge" strips along the lower edge of the roof, and be sure the roofing material (whatever it may be) laps all the way underneath the roof trim.

The roof assembly is substantial enough that it's unlikely to blow off in anything less than a hurricane. If you're concerned, though, you could include eyes and hooks to connect the base and roof section. Do be sure to leave at least 1/8" ventilation space between the two assemblies, though. We used rubber bumpers to stand the roof away from the base, but many other approaches would serve as well.

Mounting the cupola is not near as difficult as safely negotiating its considerable bulk up onto the roof. Get help for the hauling, or hire someone who's comfortable working on a steep roof. Mounting is simply a matter of sinking four 3/8" x 3" lag screws into the holes in the 2 x 4 mounting boards, through the roof, and into rafters below.

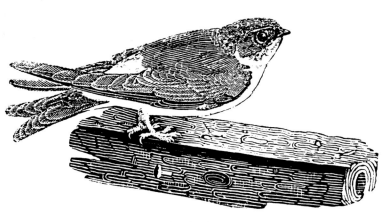

The Martin

# Colonial Townhouse

**Perfectly suited to sparrows, the 10" x 10" interior floor plan of this classic townhouse also makes excellent use of standard material sizes. Let your whimsy dictate the yard plan—perhaps you lean more toward rockers than chaize lounges—but do be sure to use waterproof glue where the base intersects the walls, and do include drain holes in the platform near the walls.**

At first glance, the detail in this bird house may seem daunting. In reality, though, the house's admittedly numerous small pieces can rapidly be mass produced by preparing stock of the right configuration and trimming off slices, as if it was a loaf of bread.

The picket fence, for example, is a piece of 1 x 3 (actual dimensions of 25/32" x 2-1/2") ripped twice on a tablesaw with the blade set at 45° to form the point. Then 3/16"-thick slices are removed from the stock on a tablesaw or with a mitre box. All 42 pickets can be produced in 15 minutes.

Likewise, the siding can be ripped from 2x (actual thickness of 1-1/2") material to allow 1" of each piece of siding to reveal. Fifteen pieces, each about 4' long, will be enough to cover all the walls of the house. They are cut carefully to fit, then glued into place from bottom to top.

Nearly all the other detail pieces in the house are formed from 1/4" stock. If you have a thickness planer, you can make your own from 1x material. A simpler solution, though, is to buy 1/4" x 1- 1/2" lattice at the lumberyard. Rip about 4 feet of this molding down to 3/4" width for the fascia on the gable ends, and then slice off about 16 feet of 1/8"-thick pieces to form the 1/8" x 1/4" stock for the rails in the picket fence and the sash dividers in the windows. Make up about 16 feet of 3/8" x 1/4" stock for the window and door casings.

Perhaps the most intimidating part of building this bird house is working at such close quarters with the tablesaw blade. This is a time to pay particular attention to the section on safety (page 30). A push stick is mandatory, and feather sticks beside and above the stock will ensure accurate results.

The lap joints in the pickets and window frames are not entirely necessary, but they make assembly much easier and add strength. You'll probably want to make these cuts with the small pieces of wood set in a larger piece of stock. Just dado a groove of the appropriate depth and width in a piece of 1 x 6 and set the tiny pieces into the groove for a run through the saw blade.

Copper makes a lovely roof, and it is quite durable, but birds would probably be just as happy with galvanized steel, which is less expensive and readily available. Your best bet for finding copper is a custom sheet-metal shop; galvanized will also be available there or at a heating and air-conditioning supply. The metal on this house is backed up by a layer of fiberboard for support. This wouldn't be necessary if the roof was permanently affixed. In this design, however, the roof was the most logical place for cleanout access. The roof attaches to the house by two studs threaded into the crossbar and passing through the roof and each chimney.

Because of the siding, the hole gets an extension donut on the outside as well as the inside. The inner one is from 3/4" plywood, while the outer is from the 3/8" wall material.

Wondering about the door? It's just a piece of tempered hardboard with a 3/4" hole filled with leftover sash parts, glued to the front wall.

## MATERIALS LIST

4' x 4' x 3/8" Plywood
2' x 2' x 3/4" Plywood
1 x 3 x 2' Fir
2 x 6 x 4' Fir
(2) 1/4" x 1-1/2" x 8' Lattice
(1) 1/4" x 1-1/16" Outside
 corner molding
2' x 2' Tempered hardboard
12" x 18" Copper (approx.
 20 gauge)
(2) 1/4"-20 x 1-1/2" Brass
 bolts and nuts
(2) No. 8 x 1-1/4"
 Roundhead woodscrews
4d Galvanized finish nails

*Colors?*

*Perhaps this one ought to go along with your own home's scheme. After all, with a little imagination you could visualize the hole as a porthole window and see children playing on the stair landing between the first and second stories.*

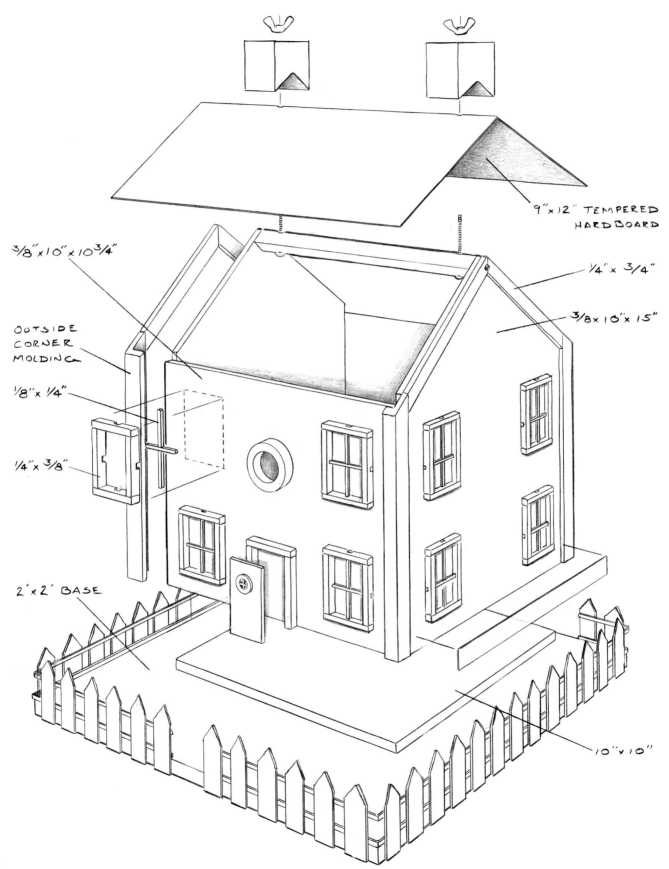

9"x12" TEMPERED HARDBOARD

3/8"x10"x10 3/4"

1/4" x 3/4"

OUTSIDE CORNER MOLDING

3/8 x 10" x 15"

1/8" x 1/4"

1/4" x 3/8"

2' x 2' BASE

10" x 10"

106

## MATERIALS LIST

1/2" x 10" x 10-1/2"
  Plywood
1/2" x 11" x 12-1/4"
  Plywood
3/4" x 10" x 10" Plywood
1/2" x 11" x 16-1/2"
  Plywood
(4) 1/4" x 3/4" x 11" Outside
  corner molding
(4) 1/4" x 3/4" x 7-3/4" Pine
1/4" x 5" x 5" Pine
2 x 2-1/4" x 7" Pine
(2) 3/8" x 1/2" x 2-1/2" Fir
(2) 3/8" x 1/2" x 4-1/2" Fir
(8) Doll house porch posts
1/4" x 2-1/2" x 5" Plywood
2 x 2-1/4" x 4-1/2" Pine
(2) 1/4" x 1-3/4" x 3"
  Plywood
3/8" x 3/8" x 2" Fir
3/8" x 3/8" x 5/8" Fir
1/2" x 1/2" x 4-1/8" Fir
1/2" x 1/2" x 1-1/2" Fir

The Little Owl

**You've heard the expression "wise as an owl." This is one school where you learn by being outside and looking in. You can put a pair (and their offspring) to work conducting ornithology classes in your own backyard.**

Based on an 11"-square box of 1/2" plywood, this bird house is simple enough in its fundamentals but offers the woodworker challenge in its details. Start by cutting out the seven basic panels. The sides are 10" x 10-1/2" (leaving 1/2" vent space at the top); the two roof panels each measure 11" x 12-1/4" and have one 11" edge beveled 45°; the floor is 3/4" x 10" x 10" plywood; and the front and back walls are 16-1/2" high, with double 45° miters to form the peak.

Before assembling these parts, bore the 3" entry hole in the front wall 4" below the peak. Then use a 4" hole saw to cut a disk of 1/4" plywood, and, from that, remove a 3" hole using the same pilot hole. Glue and clamp this ring to the entry hole to extend it outward. With that done, assemble all the walls and the roof, but leave the floor for later so you can still work from the inside.

All the vertical wall joints are covered with 1/4" x 3/4" outside corner molding, and the gable ends get 1/4" x 3/4" trim mitered to match. The same material goes around the eaves of the roof, but you should wait until trim elements are fitted before attaching this last bit of detail.

Starting from the bottom of the trim elements, the stairway is based on a piece of 2x lumber 2-1/4" high and 7" long. We suggest you assemble the whole thing on the bench and then attach it to the house with screws from the inside. The steps are 3/4" high and 3/4" wide. You can either mortise these or cut them by running the stock through flat and then on end. We picked up the turned porch posts at a doll house supply store and capped them with 3/8"-thick, 1/2" wide railings made from fir. These are mighty tiny pieces to be cutting on a table saw; you might want to consider using a small hand miter box better suited to this scale of work. The posts are centered on the steps and 3/8" in on each side of the landing. From there, the final two split the distance three ways—about 1-3/32" each, on center. The door is simply a 2-1/2" x 5" piece of 1/4" plywood. Don't let the detail scare you; it's just a combination of two different densities of gray paint.

Above the door is an awning built up on a 4-1/2"-long piece of 2 x 2-1/4" mitered to a 90° point. Again, screw this block to the front of the house from the inside. Then apply the 1-3/4" x 3" roof panels. To cover the peak, we glued on a piece of molding from the doll house supply store. The collar beam is a piece of 3/8" x 3/8" stock 2" long, and the king post is the same material about 5/8" long. Exact dimensions aren't important here; just fiddle until they fit.

At the peak of the gable end is another collar beam and king post, this time from 1/2" stock to reflect the larger scale. The former is 4-1/8" long and the latter 1-1/2". Once these are secured, you can attach the rest of the 1/4" x 3/4" molding to the roof eaves.

The final bit of fanciful detail is the belfry, a 4-1/4" piece of 2 x 2 with a mitered point. 1" holes are bored through all four sides to form the cavity for the doll house bell. (It actually rings!) After you've attached the belfry, cover the remainder of the roof peak with more doll house molding.

To complete the house, set the 3/4" plywood floor in place and bore two holes through each side and into the edge of the floor with a no.8 countersink bit. No.8 x 1" screws will hold the floor in place and allow easy removal for cleaning.

Few one-room school houses remain in use these days. In fact, modern youngsters may be at a loss to figure out what this bird house is supposed to be. If so, it's time they learned.

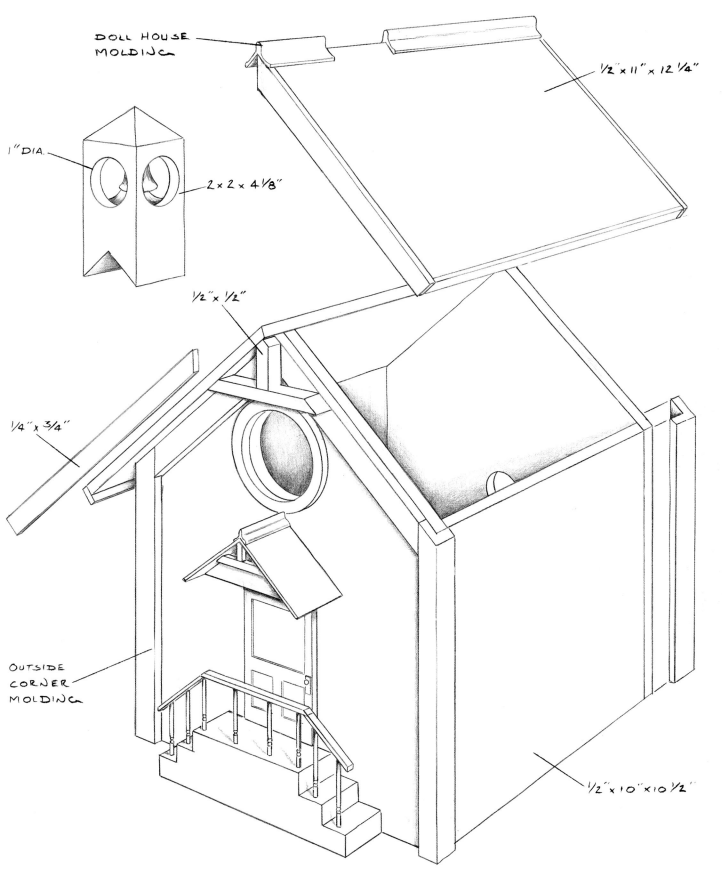

DOLL HOUSE MOLDING

1/2" x 11" x 12 1/4"

1" DIA.

2 x 2 x 4 1/8"

1/2" x 1/2"

1/4" x 3/4"

OUTSIDE CORNER MOLDING

1/2" x 10" x 10 1/2"

**109**

# Southern Mansion

**Look out Scarlet, Tara's turning condo for south bound carpet-bagging martins.**

**One of the unanticipated benefits of preparing this book has been the architectural education we've gotten trying to mimic human residences in bird scale. The Southern Mansion, for example, turned out, when reduced to its significant elements, to be an enclosed Parthenon. Not only because of its columns, just as much for its cornice and the porch below the columns, it is clearly "Greek revival."**

The core of this house is a 7-3/4"-deep, 21"-square box. The front panel overlaps the top, bottom, and sides, and has 2-1/2" holes centered 3-3/4", 10-1/2", and 17-1/4" from the bottom as well as either side. Assemble the box with glue and nails, leaving out the inset back panel at this point.

Next, prepare the dormers by cutting two 16" pieces of 2 x 6 with a 45° bevel at one end. Screw the boards to each side from the inside with no.8 x 1-1/2" woodscrews so they're flush with the bottom and the back.

Form the front porch by dadoing 1/2" steps into a 2 x 4 x 21". To allow rain to drain between the steps and the house, the 2 x 4 is doweled to the 3/4" plywood so it sets out 1/16" from the front wall. Drill three 1/2" holes 1/2" deep, centered 3/8" up the front wall and equally spaced along it. Drill corresponding holes in the 2 x 4 steps; painstaking accuracy will pay off here. Then saw off three 1-1/16" lengths of 1/2" dowel, make sure the holes are thoroughly cleaned out, and glue everything together.

The column pedestals are 2"-square pieces of 1/2" plywood. Like the parthenon feeder, the columns on this house are inset 1/4" into pedestals, top and bottom. Use a spade or auger bit to bore these 1-1/4" holes, and glue and nail four of the pedestals to the porch, positioning their left sides 1/4", 6", 12-3/4", and 18-3/4" from the left edge of the porch.

At the top, the pedestals are attached to a 2 x 2-1/2" x 21" block. Cut this piece, and glue and nail the other four pedestals in locations corresponding to those below. Next, cut the four 17-3/8" closet rod columns, glue them into the pedestals in the porch, slide the upper pedestal assembly over their tops, and screw the upper block to the front wall from the inside.

To divide the interior into 6" x 6" apartments, cut four pieces of 3/4" plywood 6-1/4" wide and 19-1/2" long. Then follow the procedure for egg-crate joining described in the Cupola. This tick-tack-toe-looking assembly slides into the box from the rear and can be secured with nails through the walls, roof, and floor into its ends. A removable 3/4" x 19-1/2" x 19-1/2" sheet of plywood closes off the back.

Roof sheathing consists of a 12" x 24" piece of 1/2" plywood glued and nailed to the top of the 3/4" plywood box. Once that's in place, trim the top with mitered 1-1/4" crown molding. Repeat this process on the dormers using 3/4" base cap molding.

We suggest that you make a full-scale mockup of the copper roof in thin cardboard before you consider putting snips to metal. The multiple slopes complicate the shape before folding, and this is a fairly big piece of material (18" x 27"). In fact, you might find cutting and folding the 3" x 6-1/2" dormer roofs a confidence-building warmup to tackling the main roof. The main roof stands 4" above the sheathing at the back and has its corner creases positioned 6" in from the left and right edges horizontally (the hypotenuse of the triangle is 7"). We found that the folds make the copper stiff enough that no support is needed underneath. Nail the copper sheets to the wood below with copper brads.

The Southern Mansion is designed to be mounted to a wall. Because of its heft, though, you'll probably want to position it low enough that you don't need more than a short step-stool to reach it for removal and cleaning. We'd suggest sinking 3/8" lag screws through your home's siding and into wall studs for security. You might bore pairs of holes in the

## MATERIALS LIST

3/4" x 21" x 21" Plywood
(2) 3/4" x 7" x 19-1/2" Plywood
(2) 3/4" x 7" x 21" Plywood
(2) 2 x 6 x 16" Pine
2 x 4 x 21" Pine
(3) 1/2" x 1-1/16" Dowels
(8) 1/2" x 2" x 2" Plywood
2 x 2-1/2" x 21" Pine
(4) 1-1/4" x 17-3/8" Closet rods
(4) 3/4" x 6-1/4" x 19-1/2" Plywood
3/4" x 19-1/2" x 19-1/2" Plywood
1/2" x 12" x 24" Plywood
5', 1-1/4" Crown molding
2', 3/4" Base cap molding
18" x 27" 18-22 ga. Copper sheets
(2) 3" x 6-1/2" 18-22 ga. Copper sheets
6d Galvanized finish nails
Copper brads
(12) no.8 x 1-1/2" Brass flathead woodscrews
(2) 3/8" x 3" Lag screws

*Paint Pointer*

***The Southern Mansion is a particularly good example of how much can be done with paint. Both the front door and the windows on the dormers are lent the impression of depth by the use of multiple shades of gray paint. Darker grays form shadows that emphasize the lighter grays of the actual elements.***

**111**

mansion's back wall—one large enough to pass over the lag screw's head just below a smaller one that fit's the screw's shank. That way you can remove it by just lifting a bit and pulling it away from the wall.

Though we imagine this house at the end of a long drive lined by live oaks festooned with Spanish moss, you shouldn't dismiss it just because you're a Yankee. If anyone asks, just say it's "Greek revival."

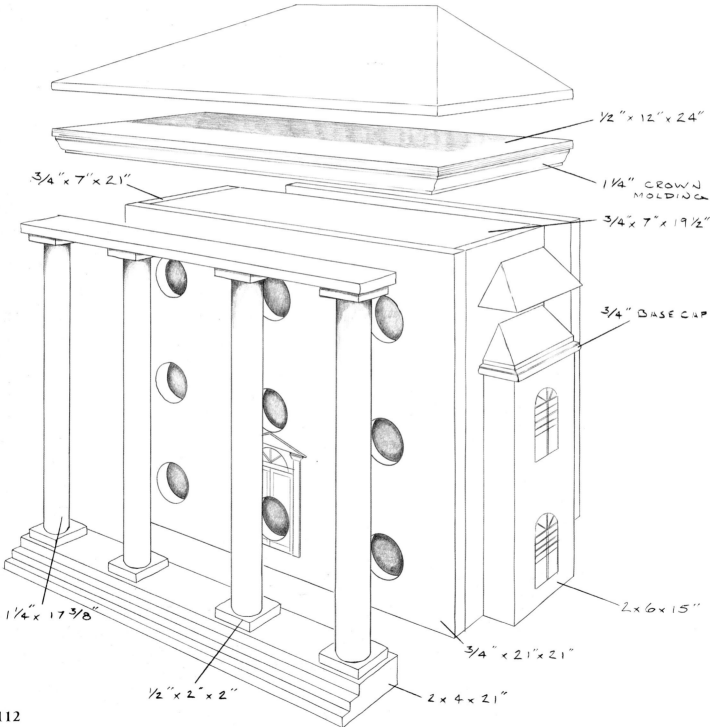

½" × 12" × 24"

1¼" CROWN MOLDING

¾" × 7" × 21"

¾" × 7" × 19½"

¾" BASE CAP

2 × 6 × 15"

1¼" × 17 3/8"

½" × 2" × 2"

¾" × 21" × 21"

2 × 4 × 21"

The Raven

## MATERIALS LIST

(4) 3/4" x 11-1/2" x 21"
   Plywood
3/4" x 11-1/2" x 11-1/2"
   Plywood
3/4" x 10" x 10" Plywood
6', 3/4" Base cap molding
2 x 4" x 7' Pine
6', 1-1/4" Picture molding
1 x 2" x 8-1/4" Pine
3-1/2" x 7-1/2" Tempered
   hardboard
(2) 8-1/4"-long Shelf edge
   molding
5"-long Shelf edge molding
(2) 1-1/4" x 1-1/4" x 2-1/2"
   Pine
(2) 1" Wooden balls
(42) 1-1/2" Wooden pegs
(2) 3/4" Wooden balls
3/16" Dowel
2 x 4" x 6-1/4" Pine
2 x 4" x 6-3/4" Pine
1 x 3-5/8" x 6" Pine
15" Doll house dental
   molding
(2) 5/8" x 8-7/8" Dowels
12" x 12" 18-22 ga. Copper
6d Galvanized finish nails
8d Galvanized finish nails
(8) no.8 x 1-1/2" Brass
   flathead woodscrews

"And the raven, never flitting, still is sitting, *still* is sitting..."-- Edgar Allen Poe

We're not sure why, but there's a bit of a sinister overtone about this bird house. Maybe it's the accentuated slope of the front stoop awning. Maybe it's the embattlements on the roof. Or maybe it's just the paint. In any event, while the look leaves us a teensy bit wary, we're confident that the sparrows aren't up on their Poe and, absent any ravens, won't object.

Beneath all the trim you'll find a basic 11-1/2"-square, 21"-high, 3/4"-plywood box with mitered corners. The top overlaps the sides, while the floor is recessed inside. At this point you can assemble all the pieces of the box except the floor.

The mansard roof is made up entirely of trim components. Starting 1/4" below the roof, we have mitered 3/4" base cap molding, followed by 2 x 4" stock beveled to leave a 1/2" thickness at the top. Depending on your tablesaw's depth capacity, you may have to work from both sides of the board to achieve the 4" bevel. Prepare about 7' of this material; you'll use it in both the front and side porch roofs.

Directly below the beveled 2x lies mitered picture molding with its back against the underside of the 2x. Spaced 1" each side of the corners are 1/2"-wide sections of crown molding that serve as corbels for the picture molding eaves.

The roof over the front stoop duplicates the mansard main roof, including the 1" taper from bottom to top. Place the 2 x 4" segment before the base cap and picture molding, positioning its bottom 9-3/4" above the base and centering it left-right in the front wall.

Next, cut a 2" x 8-1/4" piece of 1x stock and bevel three of its edges 1/4" at 45°. Screw this board to the front wall from the inside with no.8 x 1-1/2" screws. The posts are 1-1/4" x 1-1/4" x 2-1/2" with bevels at the top, and verti-

cal saw kerfs for decoration. On those go 1" balls attached with 3/16" dowel. Position these posts 3/8" in from the outer corners of the porch and nail them from underneath.

The door is made from tempered hardboard and measures 3-1/2" x 7-1/2". Glue it in place and then drill the 1-1/2" entry hole centered 6-1/4" above the bottom. To frame the door, use sections of shelf edge molding. The doorknob is a tiny bead glued to the hardboard.

The lamps that brace the front entrance consist of upside-down pegs with 3/4" wooden balls. Both of these items are available at craft stores. We mounted the lamps with 1/2" sections of 3/16" dowel drilled and glued into the pegs and the wall.

To give the side porch more authority, it's cut from 2 x 4" material, with 3/4" steps. In keeping with the motif, each step is beveled 1/4" at 45°. Drill 1/4"-deep 5/8" holes for the posts at the corners, flush to the edge of the bevel. Position the side porch 2-1/4" back from the front wall, and screw it to the wall from the inside.

The roof over the side porch is a bit more complicated than the front one. Start with a 6-3/4"-long section of the beveled 2 x 4", and set your tablesaw blade to 16°. Run each of the short edges past the blade to form the additional tapers on the roof top. Now, prepare a 3-5/8" x 6" piece of 1x. Bevel three edges of one face of this board 1/4" at 45°, and bore 1/4"-deep 5/8" holes in the corners flush with the bevel. Then glue and nail it to the 2x so it's flush with the back and recessed 3/8" from the other three edges. In this recess, miter dental molding from a doll house supply shop.

Cut two 5/8" dowels, 8-7/8" long, to support the side porch roof. Glue the dowels into the holes in the porch, and fit the roof on top of them. Holding everything square, nail and glue the porch roof to the wall from the inside.

To complete the construction, glue a 12" square sheet of copper over the top of the house, and drill holes through it and into the roof to accept the 1-1/2" pegs. These holes are 1" on center, starting 1/2" in from each corner.

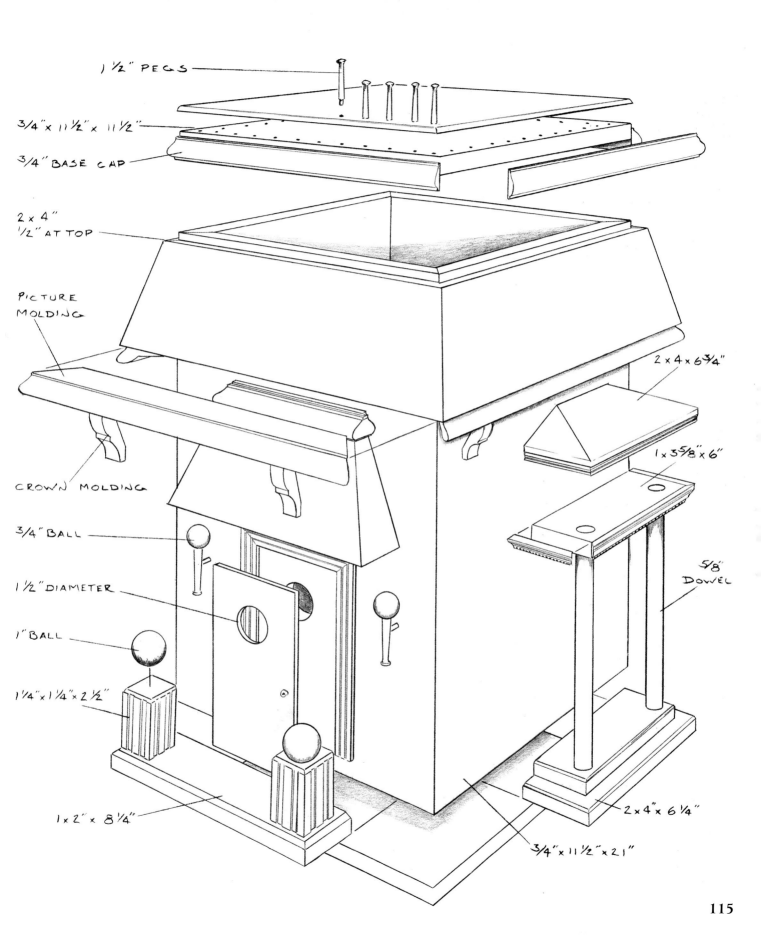

1½" PEGS

¾" x 11½" x 11½"

¾" BASE CAP

2 x 4"
½" AT TOP

PICTURE
MOLDING

2 x 4 x 6¾"

1 x 3⅝" x 6"

CROWN MOLDING

¾" BALL

1½" DIAMETER

5/8"
DOWEL

1" BALL

1¼" x 1¼" x 2½"

1 x 2" x 8¼"

2 x 4" x 6¼"

¾" x 11½" x 21"

**115**

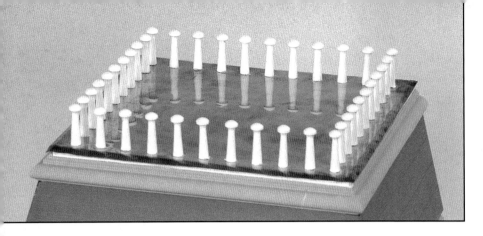

# Haunted Bird House

Glue the pegs into the roof, sealing the joint with the adhesive to prevent water from seeping in. The 10" square base should be screwed into the walls so it can be removed for cleaning. Don't forget to drill a few 1/4" drainage holes in it. Sparrows forced to stand knee deep are likely to quoth the raven, "Nevermore."

## Bedeviled Bevels

*Cutting a perfectly smooth bevel on a tablesaw is no small trick. In fact, we can't tell you how. But we can tell you how to hide an imperfect one. Start by beveling stock that's 4-1/2" wide, instead of 4". The cut face will go against the wall of the house. Once the bevel is acceptably flat, run both edges of the stock against the blade with it set to 90°. Now the sole uncut (and factory-smooth) side will face out.*

*This Victorian bird house lends a special accent to interior decor.*

The Golden-Crested Wren

**Though it's really no more complex than the Haunted Bird House or the Colonial Townhouse, this project's small scale results in the finest detail work of any in this book. But before you flip the page in panic at the thought of trying to saw 1/16" stock on a tablesaw, remember that all the tiny components in this house are available at craft and doll-house supply stores. Thus, building a row house of your own liking is more a matter of imaginative layout and pinpoint gluing than precision saw work.**

## MATERIALS LIST

(4) 3/4" x 6-1/2" 10" Plywood
3/4" x 7" x 7" Plywood
1 x 2-1/2" x 12" Pine
1 x 1-1/2" x 2-1/2" Pine
1-1/4" x 2-3/4" Tempered hardboard
1/4" x 1/4" Doll house stock
1-3/16" x 2-1/4" x 2-1/2" Pine
2x Right isosceles triangle w/ 2-3/4" base
Doll house porch posts
3/16" x 1-1/2" x 2-1/2" Pine
2', 3/4" Cove molding
30", 1/4" Quarter-round
1', 3/16" Half-round
1/16" x 1" x 12" Doll house stock
1/4" x 1/4" x 12" Doll house stock
1/16" x 1/8" x 4' Doll house stock
1/16" x 1/16" x 3' Doll house stock
6d Galvanized finish nails
(10) no. 8 x 1-1/2" Brass flathead woodscrews

Set up especially for bluebirds, but commodious for chicadees as well, the 5" x 5" floor plan is enclosed in a mitered 6-1/2"-square, 10"-high, 3/4"-plywood cylinder. On top goes a slightly oversized 7"-square roof to help emphasize the corbeling. Pick one side as the front and bore a 1-1/2" entry hole, centered 6-3/4" up and 1-3/4" from the left edge.

To form the bay windows, rip a 2-1/2"-wide, 12"-long piece of 1x, tilt the table saw blade 30°, and bevel both edges. From this stock, cut one piece 1" long and another 10" long. Glue and nail the longer one to the front of the house, so its right edge is 3/8" in from the right wall of the house. Above it, on the 3/4" plywood roof overhang, attach the 1" segment of beveled stock.

Before tackling the detail work on the bay windows, let's work on the front porch and balcony. From the bottom, building upward, the porch is a 1-1/2" x 2-1/2" piece of 1x with 3/8" steps. Screw it to the front wall from the inside, set in 3/8" from the left wall. The front door is 1-1/4" x 2-3/4" tempered hardboard, with 7/8" squares of 1/16" doll house stock for panels. A copper nail, not quite set, does a good imitation of a door knob while helping to hold things together. Door casings are 1/4" stock, mitered at the corners.

We used turned doll house porch posts cut down to 2-3/4" to support the balcony. That part, however, is rendered from a piece of pine

that started out as a 1-3/16" x 2-1/4" x 2-1/2" block. First, set the saw blade to 45° and a height of 3/4". With the rip fence set 9/16" from the base of the blade, run a 1-3/16" x 2-1/2" face through in both directions to remove a V on the underside of the balcony. Next, return to vertical, mount a 3/4" dado, set its depth to 3/4", and readjust the fence to keep it 9/16" from the cutting edge. Run the side of the stock opposite the V through in both directions to remove a total width of 1-3/8", leaving 9/16" on each side. Now, turn the stock so the V notch is up and running perpendicular to the blade, and run the wood through the saw again. Then flip it, keeping the same face against the fence, and repeat. To finish the balcony, lower the dado to a height of 1/8", and repeat the process on the front, so the square posts are revealed. Mount the finished piece 3/8" from the left wall, so its floor is 5" up.

Two more 2" posts support the triangular balcony roof. That piece is an isosceles right triangle of 2x lumber with a 2-3/4" base. Center it on the posts and run a screw in from behind. Then add the beveled 3/16" x 1-1/2" x 2-1/2" roof panels.

At this point, you can start to add trim. If you happen to have a power miter box, this would be a great time to get it out. Otherwise a hand miter box, tablesaw, or radial arm saw will do. From the top, there's 3/4" mitered cove molding attached to the edge of the roof, and then 1/4" quarter-round just below it. The other two bands that go all the way around the house are 3/4" shelf edge molding.

From here you can take the detail as far as your fancy leads you. We'll briefly describe what we've done to give you some ideas. Bear in mind that all of the following components came from a craft store, and there's even more there to choose from. The bay windows were all assembled piece-by-piece from 1/16"-thick material; the window frames are 1/8" wide, while the sashes are 1/16"; the panels above and below are 3/4" square. Mitered 1/4" quarter-round sits right above the upper windows. The sills below both are 3/16" half-round.

119

## Entry Options

**As complicated as the detail work is on this house, one has to wonder if a bird will find the way in. Consider placing the entry hole on the side or back, either of which presents a less-imposing egress.**

Ornamentation on the balcony includes 1/4" quarter-round over the V, and 1/4"-square railings mitered together.

Copper protects the flat roof of our row house. This can be effectively formed in place. Cut out the shape of the roof, adding 1/4" all around. Lay it onto the roof and begin to fold the edges over. At the outside corners, slit the copper with snips so it can overlap; snip it at inside corners so it can open slightly. Once you get the copper overlapped evenly and squarely, tack the edges to the plywood with copper brads.

Because of the trim around the foundation of the house, it would be difficult to inset a floor. Therefore, we suggest you screw a base to the house from underneath, so it can be removed for cleaning. Otherwise, consider dividing the back wall in half horizontally (with a beveled cut) and screwing the lower portion in place so it can be removed. Likewise, a few ventilation holes high in the back would probably be welcomed by the occupants.

In the end, the tiny details of this house are what set it apart—they are the accomplishment. The only problem is: who wants to set this house out next to a pasture on a fencepost, far from admiring eyes?

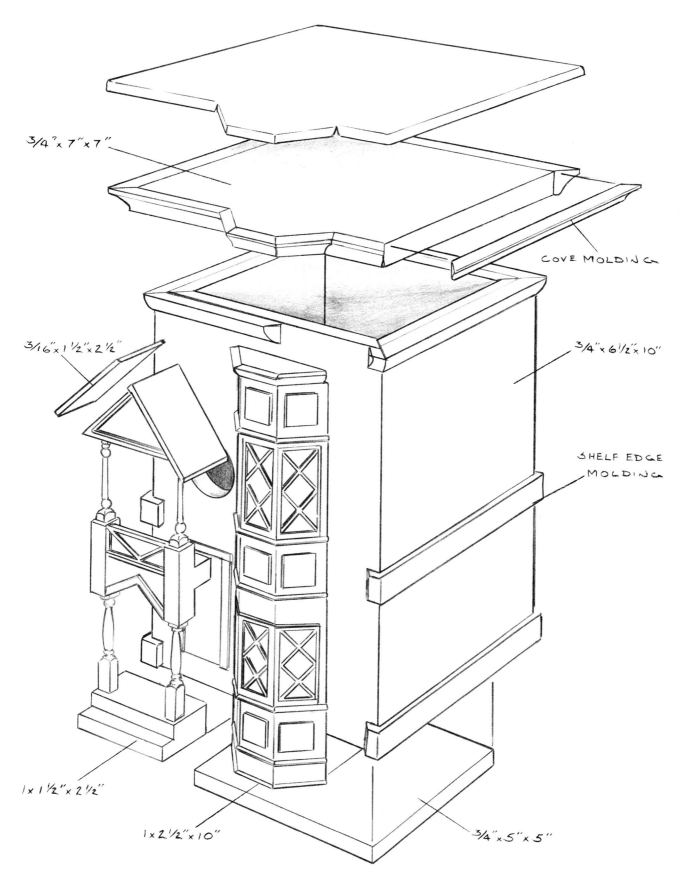

3/4" x 7" x 7"

COVE MOLDING

3/16" x 1 1/2" x 2 1/2"

3/4" x 6 1/2" x 10"

SHELF EDGE
MOLDING

1 x 1 1/2" x 2 1/2"

1 x 2 1/2" x 10"

3/4" x 5" x 5"

**121**

# Fifties Tract Home

In the aftermath of World War II, the American dream of home ownership became a reality for many because of the suburban tract house. Simple boxes distinguished from one another mainly by variations in paint and details, the description "cookie cutter homes" was often apt. Our problem is that, to our knowledge, this is the only avian tract house in existence. Arguably, we shouldn't call it a tract house—not until you get busy and build a bevy of duplicates.

*Landscaping*

*While unbroken lawn is certainly appropriate for the Fifties Tract Home, we were tempted to indulge ourselves at the craft store. If you haven't looked into the materials available for decorating model railroads and doll houses, you're in for a side trip through fantasy land. Don't let our austerity hold you back.*

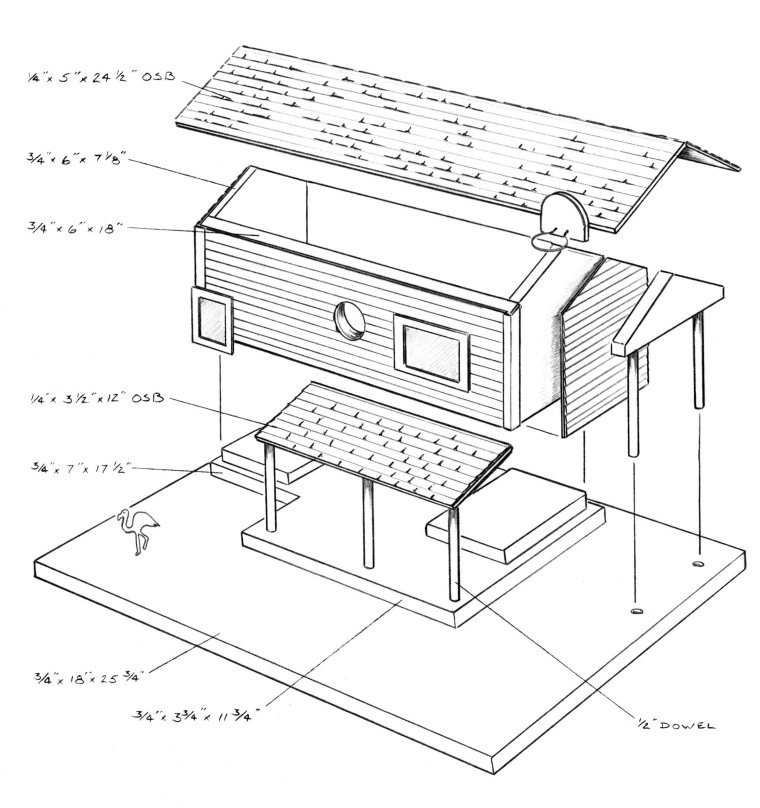

¼″ x 5″ x 24 ½″ OSB

¾″ x 6″ x 7⅛″

¾″ x 6″ x 18″

¼″ x 3½″ x 12″ OSB

¾″ x 7″ x 17 ½″

¾″ x 18″ x 25 ¾″

¾″ x 3¾″ x 11 ¾″

½″ DOWEL

# Fifties Tract Home

Appropriately enough, plywood is the motif for this bird house. Its base, incorporating the yard and driveway, is 3/4" x 18" x 25-3/4". Atop that goes the foundation, a 3/4" x 7" x 17-1/2" piece, and the front porch, measuring 3/4" x 3-3/4" x 11-3/4". Position the foundation about 1-1/4" in from the left rear corner of the base; the porch, of course, goes in front of and flush with the right side of the foundation.

At this point drill four or five 1/4" holes through the foundation and base in the "bedroom" for drainage. Then chuck your 1/2" bit and bore two 1/4" deep holes centered 3/4" in from each front corner of the porch, one centered 3/4" back from the front and in the middle left-right, and two more centered 1-1/2" from the right side of the base and 2" and 7-1/2" from the back. These holes will accommodate the 1/2" dowels that support the porch roof and carport.

Because the walls overlap the foundation by 1/4", it's helpful to have nailers inside. These consist of 3/4" x 5-1/4" x 6" plywood squares at each end of the house, set back from the edge of the foundation 1/2" with their long dimension front to back. The two end walls and the partitions that form the 6"-square chamber inside are 3/4" x 6" x 7-1/8" boards with the roof slope of about 20° mitered into their tops. The same angle is beveled onto the top of the 3/4" x 6" x 18" front and back walls. Attach the two end walls and the front wall to the nailers inside using 6d galvanized finish nails and glue. Affix the back wall with no.8 x 1-1/4" brass flathead woodscrews so it can be removed for cleaning.

We confess to committing an anachronism in building the roof. Oriented strand board wasn't around in the fifties, but we're convinced builders would have jumped to use it had it been available. The two roof sections measure 1/4" x 5" x 24-1/2", and are beveled to the roof slope on one long edge. While you're cutting OSB, go ahead and prepare a 3-1/2" x 12" piece for the porch roof.

To support the roof over the carport, cut a 3" x 7-1/2" gable from 3/4" plywood. Drill 1/4"-deep 1/2" holes in one long edge of this board, centered 1-1/4" x 5-3/4" from one end. Next, miter the other side to match the roof slope. With glue, insert 1/2" x 6-1/2" dowels into the holes in the gable end and then insert the assembly into the base. To complete the roof installation, nail the OSB to the tops of the walls (not the back one) and the gable end with 4d galvanized finish nails.

The bevel lap siding comes from a doll house supply store, as does the 1/16" x 3/8" material for the corner posts. Fasteners aren't necessary with these materials; just glue them in place. Once the glue has set, go ahead and drill the 2" entry hole in the front wall 3" up from the bottom. The windows consist of a frame made from 1/16" stock enclosing unexposed pieces of black-and-white photographic film. These may not prove to be durable over time, but hardier substitutes are available at the doll house supply.

To support the porch roof, cut three 1/2" x 5-1/4" dowels and glue them into the holes in the porch floor. Then tack the porch roof to the tops of the posts and to the wall of the house from the inside. Only a small slope is called for here. We covered our house's roofs with doll house asphalt shingles. They come in rolls, so they're not quite as tedious to install as they might first look.

The rest of the ornamentation pretty much speaks for itself. Perhaps you'd prefer plastic deer to the flamingos. A tiny bird bath would add an ironic touch. Colors, too, are a matter of whim. Just remember, we've got the only robin's egg blue house on the block.

## MATERIALS LIST

3/4" x 18" x 5-3/4" Plywood
3/4" x 7" x 17-1/2" Plywood
3/4" x 3-3/4" x 11-3/4" Plywood
(2) 3/4" x 5-1/4" x 6" Plywood
(4) 3/4" x 6" x 7-1/8" Plywood
(2) 3/4" x 6" x 18" Plywood
(2) 1/4" x 5" x 24-1/2" OSB
1/4" x 3-1/2" x 12" OSB
3/4" x 3" x 7-1/2" Plywood
(2) 1/2" x 6-1/2" Dowels
Doll house siding
Doll house trim
Doll house shingles
Assorted knickknacks
6d Galvanized finish nails
4d Galvanized finish nails
(4) no.8 x 1-1/4" Brass flathead woodscrews

The Goldfinch

*A phosphorescent strip tacked to the eaves creates a neon effect at dusk.*

# Fly-by-Night Motel

Since it lacks a heated pool or waterbeds, the automobile association might rate our motel as only a one-star accommodation. But we think passing purple martins will find the fly-up convenience hard to resist. Who knows, they may even ask for weekly rates. Offering neighborly yet decently private housing for these most congenial nesting birds, this 50s-era, mom-and-pop flytel will liven up your yard, as will its occupants.

# Fly-by-Night Motel

## MATERIALS LIST

(2) 3/4" x 6" X 7" X 7-1/2"
   Plywood
(5) 3/4" x 6" x 6-1/4" x
   6-3/4" Plywood
3/4" x 6-3/4" x 21" Plywood
3/4" x 6-3/4" x 27-3/4"
   Plywood
3/4" x 7-5/8" x 14-1/4"
   Plywood
3/4" x 7-5/8" x 21" Plywood
3/4" x 6" x 19-1/2" x 26-1/4"
   Plywood

The house is basically an L-shaped 3/4" plywood box with ornamentation. The only complication is the roof slope, which requires bevel and miter cuts of about 5°. The simplest approach here is to cut the end and partition walls first, and then trim the front and back walls to fit. Prepare two end walls and five partitions. The end walls measure 6" on the base, 7" on one vertical, and 7-1/2" on the other, while the partitions are 3/4" shorter (6" x 6-1/4" x 6-3/4") to butt against the base.

Next, cut out a 4'2" length of 3/4" ply 6-3/4" wide, with a 5° bevel along one edge. Then, set the saw blade back to square and rip off a 3' length about 7-5/8" wide (leaving the 5°

bevel from the last cut on one edge). Now check the short face of the front wall and the tall face of the back wall against an end wall to see that the bevels and miter cuts all match up perfectly. Trim until they do. Once they're just the right size, crosscut the back wall with the blade set at 45° to form pieces 21" and 27-3/4" long, and the front wall at the same bevel to form pieces 14-1/4" and 21" long. The bevel cuts form miter joints at the corners.

Now drill the 2-1/2" entry holes in the front walls at points centered 3" from the bottom, and 4" and 10-1/2" from the outer end of the short section, then 2-1/2", 10-1/2", and 17" from the outer end of the long section. At this point, you could also add an entry hole in back

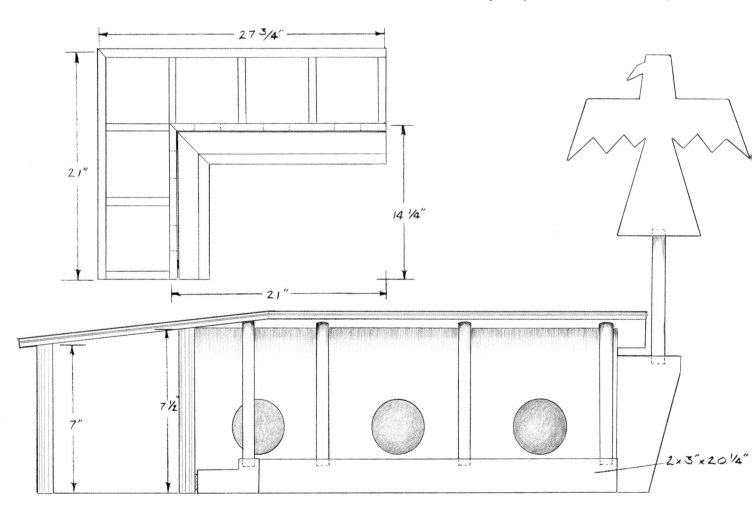

to access the "room" at the corner. (Perhaps it can be the manager's quarters.)

The sidewalk is cut from 2x fir 3" wide, with a 1/2" x 2" chunk removed from the top. Prepare about 3'6" of the material and then cut one piece 13-1/2" long and another 20-1/4" long, mitered so they meet at the inside corner. Place shims about 1/16" thick every 6" or so between the walkways and the front walls before you nail them from the inside with 8d galvanized finish nails. The gap will allow water to drain through, rather than pooling.

One more piece needs to be attached before assembling the walls of the house. The standard for the sign is a 6" length of the same 2 x 3" stock used for the walkway. We tapered it to 1-1/2" width at the bottom, starting about an inch below the top. Attach the standard from the inside of the end wall using two no.8 x 1-1/2" brass flathead woodscrews.

The base of the bird house is a 6" x 19-1/2" x 26-1/4" L of 3/4" plywood that fits inside all the exterior walls. Once you've cut it out, you can assemble the walls and partitions around and atop it with glue and 6d nails. Don't, however, attach the base to the walls and partitions permanently. Countersink no.8 x 1-1/2" woodscrews at strategic points so the base can be removed for cleaning.

Two roof panels from 1/4" oriented strand board are needed to accommodate the twin roof slopes. Both are 12" wide; one is 23" long, the other 30". Miter one end of each at 45° so they can meet. Before you secure the roof, cut five 6-1/2" posts from 5/8" dowel, mitering one end at 5° to match the roof slope. Cut the heads off five 4d finish nails and push the cut off ends into the square ends of the dowels. Apply glue sparingly to ends with the nails and space them evenly along the walkway, pushing the nails into the walkway to hold the dowels while the glue sets. Go ahead and position the roof panels, leaving 1/2" overhang at the back, and tack them to the walls and the dowels with 4d galvanized finished nails. Plain-old black roll roofing makes a suitable and effective cover for this 50s throwback.

All that's left is the sign itself. Refer to the diagram and your own creativity to shape a 6" or 8" piece of 2 x 6 fir into the appropriate caricature. Anyone who's been around more than a couple of decades and has traveled must have their own renditions of the thunderbird imprinted in memory. For the birds, though, this combination of pigeon perch and predator ought to be a whole new treat.

2 x 3" x 13-1/2" Fir
2 x 3" x 20-1/4" Fir
2 x 3" x 6" Fir
1/4" x 12" x 23" OSB
1/4" x 12" x 30" OSB
(6) 5/8" x 6-1/2" Dowels
Roll roofing
2 x 6 x 6" Fir
8d Galvanzied finish nails
6d Galvanized finish nails
4d Galvanized finish nails
no. 8 x 1-1/2" Brass flathead
   woodscrews

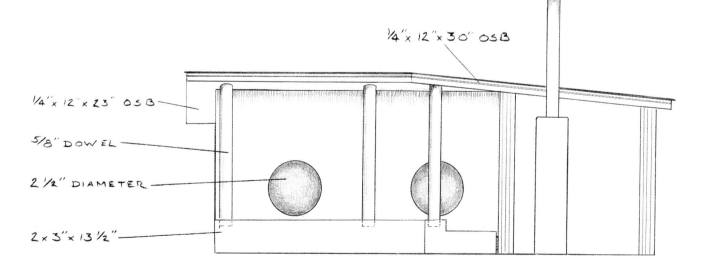

## MATERIALS LIST

(2) 3/4" X 7-1/2" X 16"
    Plywood
(2) 3/4" x 5-1/4" x 16"
    Plywood
3/4" x 6" x 7-1/2" Plywood
2 x 10-1/2" x 10-1/2" Pine
(2) 1/2" x 8-1/2" x 8-1/2"
    Plywood
1" x 7" Dowel
1" x 3-1/4" Dowel
(2) 1 x 1-3/4" x 1-3/4" Pine
(18) Button screw hole plugs
(2) no.6 x 1-1/4" Brass
    flathead woodscrews
14" x 16" 18-22 ga. Copper
    sheet
Copper brads

*"Keep a green tree in
your heart and perhaps
the singing bird will
come."—anonymous
Chinese proverb*

# Postmodern Dwelling

**While there may not be a distinctly "modern" period in bird house architecture to react to, we still think this rendition earns its title by setting aside the tedious functionalism common to most bird house designs. Equally well suited to pileated woodpeckers or (with the addition of an interior ramp) wood ducks, this house is, at the least, postboring.**

The Postmodern is one of the easiest projects in this book, consisting of a 16"-high box of 3/4" plywood, a top and bottom, and some ornamentation. Start by cutting the 5-1/4" sides and the 7-1/2"-wide front and back. Then cut out another piece of 3/4" plywood 6" x 7-1/2".

Fit your drill with a 4" hole saw and bore holes in the 6" x 2-1/2" and one 5-1/4" x 7-1/2" panel at points centered 4" down from the tops. Then remove 2" from the 6" board to leave a semicircle. Nail the box together, butting the 5-1/4" walls into the 7-1/2" ones, and nail the 4" board to the front so its semicircle conforms to the 4" hole.

The base is a piece of 2 x 12 bevel cut at 45° to yield a 10-1/2" square. Cut another piece of 2x to form a 5-1/4" square and nail it in the center of the smaller face of the 10-1/2" piece. This board will slide inside the bottom of the house, and screws will allow it to be removed for cleaning.

Up top go two 8-1/2" squares of 1/2" plywood, again bevel cut to 45°. Nail one to the top of the walls with its bevels down, and then top it with the other, bevels up. The copper pyramid roof can be tacked to the upper piece of plywood with copper brads.

The remainder of the house's trim consists of some 1" dowel ripped in half, two 1 x 1-3/4" x 1-3/4" blocks, and button screw hole plugs. Position the half dowels 3/8" in from the edge, so they'll be centered in the 1-3/4" rectangular trim. Attach the two square blocks with no.6 x 1-1/4" brass flathead woodscrews, and cover them with the plugs.

Drill shallow holes to fit the remainder of the decorative button screw hole plugs. Center the outside ones 7/8" in from the edge. The inner two divide the distance between the outer two into three equal parts—about 1-29/32" as it happens.

When it comes to paint, this design begs for bright colors. However, recognizing that bird taste—and particularly that of wood ducks and pileated woodpeckers—may be at variance with our own, we went pastel. Likely enough, though, like humans, given a little time, they'll adapt to new styles.

The Pied Woodpecker

# Thatched Yurt

Asian nomads developed a distinctive round house that was collapsible and featured a domed or conical roof. This design lends itself beautifully to the use of natural materials, and is sure to enhance your outdoor site.

## Materials List

|   | |
|---|---|
| | *3/8" x 6" dia. Plywood* |
| 8 | *3/8" x 2-1/2" x 5-3/4" Bark-faced pine slats* |
| | *1/2" x 18" Green twig, de-barked* |
| | *1-1/2" dia. x 20" Bundle of straw* |
| | *3/16" x 10' Grapevine* |
| | *12' Thin vine or twine* |
| | *Tie wire* |

**Step One** Drill eight 3/16" holes around the perimeter of the 6" plywood circle, equidistant and 3/8" from the edge. The eight slats can be split off of a pine log to a thickness of 3/8"–1/2", then trimmed into 2-1/2" x 5-3/4" rectangles. You may gently whittle and sand the bark for a rounded look if you wish. Drill two 3/16" holes in each slat, about 3/4" from each short edge.

**Step Two** Weave a 6" dia. wreath and a 7" dia. wreath out of grapevine. The larger wreath surrounds the bottom rim of the bucket, while the smaller wreath fits inside the top rim. Using thin vine or twine, attach each slat to the plywood circle through their matching holes and around the larger wreath, wrapping your way around the rim. Lash the tops of the slats to the smaller wreath in a similar way. Cut the door hole between two slats with a coping saw, then tack a strip across the threshold cut from pine scrap.

**Step Three** With a sharp knife or hatchet, split the 18" twig into quarters 7-1/2" into one end. Fan these out into rafters and wire them securely to the bucket rim. Each rafter should extend 1" over the rim. Wire the remaining grapevine to the rafter ends to form eaves, then continue spiralling it up to form a conical frame, wiring it to the rafters as you go.

**Step Four** The bundle of straw surrounds the post, then fans out over the roof frame. Hold it in place with rubber bands around the post, then tie and wrap with thin vine or twine from the top down. Tie it down through to the frame as you spiral out over the straw, then around the eaves. Clip off the rubber bands. Trim the excess straw around the eaves with heavy scissors. A top loop can be woven as a wreath through a hole drilled through the post top for hanging.

# Mosaic Twig Treehouse

This woodsy cottage belongs up in the trees amidst breezy boughs. It can be sized to suit many species of birds, and decorated with whatever patterns your twigs inspire.

## Materials List

| | |
|---|---|
| 2 | *1 x 10" x 15" Wood planks* |
| | *1 x 10" x 10" Wood plank* |
| 2 | *1 x 8-1/2" x 10" Wood planks* |
| 2 | *3/8" x 9" x 13" Plywood* |
| | *Assorted twigs* |
| 28 | *1" dia. x 9" Bamboo* |
| 2 | *Tin cans* |
| | *10'–16' Multi-pronged trunk post* |
| | *Glue and assorted nails* |

**Step One** The chamber can be constructed out of most any 3/4" stock, preferably rough-sawn for a rustic look. Cut the roof peak out of both 10" x 15" planks at once leaving 10" corner edges. Cut an entry hole in one of these.

**Step Two** Glue and nail the 8-1/2" x 10" side planks to these to form the walls, lapping the larger planks over the smaller ones. Let dry, then glue and nail the 10" x 10" base plank to the bottom edges.

**Step Three** The shape of the twigs you find may help determine the patterns you add to the walls. The distinctively curved corner braces used on the front of this house are two halves of the same twig, carefully sawed in half. The fence pattern and door frame are split twigs cut and bent to fit, then tacked into place. Pre-drilling the nail holes will prevent splitting the twigs. A Y-shaped twig is glued into a hole drilled below the door for the perch.

**Step Four** The remaining walls can be decorated with twig mosaics. You may want to sketch a pattern on the wall before tacking the larger split twigs on to outline a particular shape, such as a star. Smaller twigs, perhaps of contrasting color, can then be cut to fit inside and around the outline and tacked into place.

**Step Five** If you plan to permanently attach your house to a post, install a lag screw through the floor and into the post before affixing the roof. If your post is multi-pronged, top nail the other flush-cut branches through the floor as well.

**Step Six** Cut 9" lengths of bamboo between the knuckles and split them in half. Pre-drill and nail a row of upturned halves on each plywood roof panel. Then pre-drill and nail rows of downturned halves over these, lapped like a tile roof.

**Step Seven** Pre-drill and nail the roof panels on top of the chamber. Open and flatten two tin cans. Bend them lengthwise to conform to the roof ridge, then pre-drill and nail them in place.

# Thunderbird Tipi

Who's to say that certain native species wouldn't want to emulate the habitats of their human counterparts. A child could have lots of fun making and decorating this piece, then waiting to see who sets up camp.

## Materials List

      *1 x 9-3/4" dia. Pine base*

7  *1/4" x 15"–16" Dowels*

      *1/4" x 6" Dowel*

      *1/4" x 2-1/8" Dowel*

      *1/4" x 1-3/4" Dowel*

      *11-1/2" x 23" Canvas*

      *String*

      *Painter's caulk*

      *Glue*

**Step One** After cutting the circular pine base, drill seven 1/4" holes about 5/8" from the edge. They should be somewhat evenly spaced, about 1/2" deep, and angled slightly toward the center. They can be widened as necessary to accommodate the tipi poles.

**Step Two** Make diagonal cuts on one end of each of the seven poles, plus the 6" dowel. This creates a more natural effect. You may even prefer to use straight branches instead of storebought dowels.

**Step Three** Glue three of the poles into somewhat evenly spaced holes, and tie them together with string about 4" from the top, before the glue dries. Glue in and tie the remaining four poles in the same manner, then the 6" dowel that supports the top flap. Squirt glue all around the top lashing to secure the juncture. Let dry.

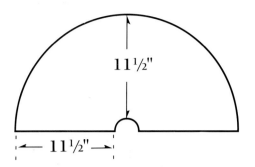

**Step Four** Cut a semicircle from the canvas as shown in the diagram. Save the scrap. Try wrapping the canvas around the poles, check for fit, and trim as necessary. There should be ample canvas touching the base to glue a seam.

**Step Five** Run a bead of glue around the base where the canvas skirt will rest. Run beads of glue down the outside of each pole and around the top lashing. Lay the canvas gently around the frame, and gently press it down over all the glue seam. Run a wide bead of glue inside the overlapping edge, then press it gently closed. Let dry.

**Step Six** Opposite the vertical seam, cut a 1-1/4" x 1-3/4" oval door, 2" from the bottom. Cut a 3" x 4" triangular flap from the scrap canvas, then glue it over the 6" dowel and onto the tipi wall. Cut a 1" x 2-1/2" panel of scrap canvas, then glue it as a V-shaped awning over the door hole. Let dry.

**Step Seven** Indent one end of the 2-1/8" dowel with a round file. Glue and nail the 1-3/4" dowel to this end to form the perch. Drill a 1/4" hole in front of the door, and glue it in place.

**Step Eight** Caulk the entire apex of the tipi, including the flap, as well as the door awning, vertical seam and base seam. Let dry. Prime and paint the entire piece with exterior grade paint. Designs can be painted on with hobby enamels. A feathered spear and other toy accessories can be added.

# Bat House

Bats aren't birds, but mammals that can devour 500 insects per minute! They're harmless to humans, yet becoming endangered. A house this size can sleep a colony of up to 30 bats. This is a fun project for kids to help with.

## Materials List

2  *1 x 12 x 15" Pine*
2  *1 x 12 x 9" Pine*
   *1 x 10-1/2" x 15" Pine*
2  *1 x 12 x 13-7/8" Pine*
   *1 x 4 x 34" Pine*
   *1/2" x 14" x 25" Plywood*
   *Glue and assorted nails*
   *2-1/2" Bolt and nut*

**Step One** You may want to use cedar for the box (painted blue in the photo) instead of pine, for better weather resistance. First cut 3/4" dado grooves lengthwise into the 12 x 9" side panels. There should be two 3/16" deep grooves on 3" centers to channel the inner partitions. Next, cut 3/16" deep grooves about 1" apart, lengthwise across one of the 12 x 15" panels (not shown in photo). Do this again with both 12 x 13-7/8" partition panels.

**Step Two** Glue and nail the 12 x 15" panels to the 12 x 9" sides, butting the corners, with all grooves facing inward. Glue and nail the 10-1/2" x 15" roof snugly on top. All seams should be tight to prevent leaks. Let dry.

**Step Three** Cut a 21" length of 1 x 4 for the tree mount. You may wish to jigsaw a bat head outline at one end and tail at the other, as in the photo. Bevel cut the remaining 13" of 1 x 4 as a mounting shim. Glue and nail the shim to the center of the tree mount, bevels up. Glue and nail the box to the center of the shim. This double seam can be reinforced with a 2-1/2" bolt through all three boards up toward the lid (not shown in photo).

**Step Four** Paint both partitions and the box interior flat black. Glue and nail the partitions into the dadoed grooves. They will be flush with the bottom of the box (unlike the photo, which has an angled roof).

**Step Five** Cut a bat silhouette from 1/2" plywood. Paint it well to seal the laminations. Paint the entire structure as you wish, then glue and nail the bat emblem proudly on the house.

# Bats in the Belfry

Here's an elegant way to control your insect population, even if your neighbors think you're a little batty. Try mounting this in a shady spot near a garden.

## Materials List

| | |
|---|---|
| 4 | *1 x 11-1/4" x 24" Pine* |
| 2 | *1 x 10-1/2" x 14-1/2" Pine* |
| | *1 x 10-1/2" x 10-1/2" Pine* |
| 4 | *13-1/2" Triangles of 1/4" plywood* |
| | *54" of 1-1/2" Decorative molding* |
| | *Floor flange* |
| | *1/2" x 3/4" x 10-1/2" Pine* |
| | *Bell* |
| | *Lathe-turned spire* |
| | *Glue and assorted finishing nails* |

**Step One** Each of the wall panels could be solid 1 x 12, two planks of 1 x 8, or 3/4" plywood. The overall dimensions can also be varied, along with corresponding adjustments for interior panels. After cutting the four wall panels, use a jigsaw to cut the window openings. The flat bottom sill should be 8" below the top edge. Mark the semi-circular arc with a compass. These windows measure 6" x 6", and should be 3/8" off-center.

**Step Two** Cut the two interior panels of solid 1 x or 3/4" plywood to fit snugly inside whatever sized chamber you're building. These can be inserted and nailed into place as simple butt joints or into dado cut grooves. Since these panels will partition the three sleeping compartments, be sure to rip cut horizontal grooves on both sides to facilitate the bat's foothold. Grooves that are about 1/8" deep and wide should be spaced 1–2" apart, and should be cut on the facing interior walls also.

**Step Three** Cut the square panel that forms the roof of the compartment to fit, either butted or dadoed into place. A standard 1" floor flange can be screwed onto the center of this panel. This will accommodate a 1" steel pipe, threaded at the top end, which can be used as the mounting post. The method used here utilized a 1-1/4" dowel post which is inserted into a 1-1/4" hole cut halfway into the roof panel. It is stabilized by a 3-1/4" square block with a 1-1/4" hole. The block slips down the dowel and is glued into place, flush with the bottom edge of the interior panels, into which it snugly fits. Use a hole saw to cut the holes.

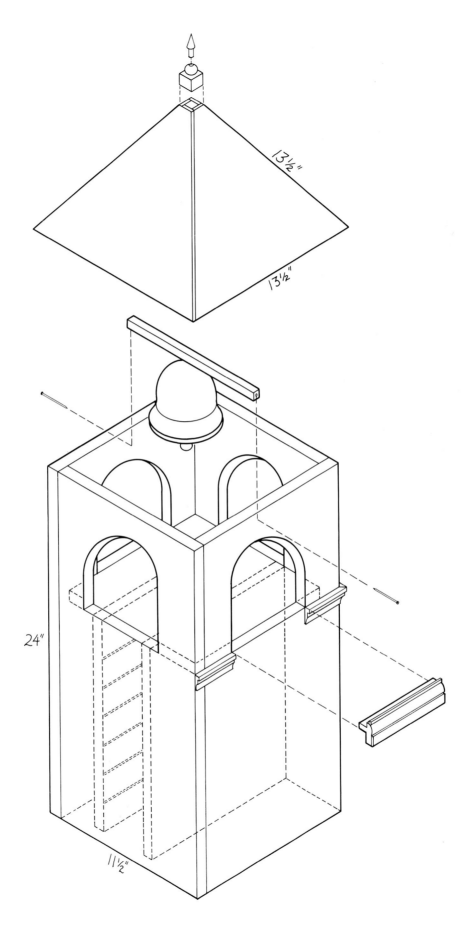

13½"

13½"

24"

11½"

141

**Step Four** Join the wall panels one corner at a time with glue and nails. Before attaching the last wall panel, insert the roof panel and secure it with glue and nails. Join the last wall, let dry, then sand all corner seams.

**Step Five** Insert the two interior panels, and secure them with glue and nails. Rip cut the 1/2" x 3/4" pine bell support, then cut a length to fit the top inside of the belfry. Find an old bell, or turn one from wood on a lathe like this one. Attach it to the support, then install the assembly with glue and nails.

**Step Six** Measure and cut the decorative molding to form the four cornices. It is wise to cut the miters first, hold them in place to mark the window edges, then make the straight cuts. Glue and nail them into place along a pre-marked horizontal line. The four sill moldings can be cut from the same molding and turned upside down, or from different molding. Cut and install these in the same manner.

**Step Seven** Cut the four 13-1/2" equilateral triangles that form the roof from 1/4" plywood. The edges that will join can either be miter cut or bevel cut for butt joints. If you choose to insert a block (as shown in the photo), bevel cut the top corners to fit. Otherwise, you can simply drill a hole in the finished roof to accept a dowel spire. To join the roof, run a bead of glue or silicone sealant on one upper edge of each panel, then lean them together and let dry. The seams can be reinforced by lightly tapping small brads into the joints, or gluing dowels or beveled strips into the inside seams.

**Step Eight** The spire can be lathe-turned, composed of doll house fittings, carved, or a sharpened dowel with beads threaded over it. Whatever its size and shape, it will be glued and nailed into a corresponding hole at the apex of the roof. This roof has a faux copper finish, but the color scheme is up to you. The finished roof assembly is glued and nailed atop the belfry. The top wall edges can be beveled for a stronger glue seam if you wish.

# Honeymoon Hideaway

The urge to hole up in this birdie bunga-
low will prove irresistible to the nesting
instincts of all true love birds. And you
won't mind cleaning up after each mating
season using the handy pull-out drawer.

## Materials List

2   *1 x 5-1/2" x 9" Pine*
    *1 x 7-1/2" x 8" Pine*
    *1 x 6-3/4" x 8" Pine*
    *1 x 3-7/8" x 5-1/2" Pine*
2   *1/2" x 7-5/8" x 12-3/4" Plywood*
    *1/4" x 4" x 6" Plywood*
3   *1/4" x 2-3/8" x 5-1/8" Plywood*
    *1/4" x 2-1/2" x 3-1/2" Plywood*
2   *5-7/8" 1/4-Round molding*
    *1/4" Lath scrap*
    *1/4" x 3" Dowel*
2   *Eyescrews*
    *Glue and assorted nails*

**Step One** Cut tapered bevels on both long edges of the 3-7/8" x 5-1/2" base block at 80°. Cut an 80° bevel on one short edge of each of the 5-1/2" x 9" side panels. Cut a tapered bevel at 60° on the opposite short sides.

**Step Two** Mark and cut the elongated pentagons from 1/2" plywood, following the diagram. In one pentagon, cut a 1-5/8" hole upper center with a hole saw. Then cut the bottom third off, 4" from the bottom, for the drawer panel.

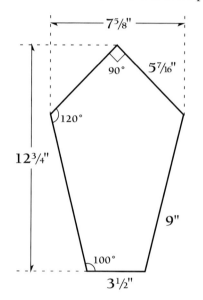

**Step Three** Glue and nail the whole pentagon to the base and sides, then join the upper pentagon section to this assembly. Glue and nail the 8" pine roof panels with a butt joint, then glue and nail the roof to the top of the chamber.

**Step Four** Cut 80° tapered bevels on both long edges of one 2-3/8" x 5-1/8" plywood panel (drawer bottom). Cut an 80° bevel on one long edge of the other two panels (drawer sides). Taper cut the 2-1/2" x 3-1/2" plywood (drawer back) so that the bottom edge measures 2-5/16". Glue these panels to the lower pentagon face, forming the drawer. Reinforce with brads after the glue is dry.

**Step Five** Cut the 1/4" lath scrap into 1/2" widths for fence and shutter slats. The same can be used for cross pieces. Cut picket points on the fencing, and attach as you wish. The windows can be painted on. Cut more scrap for the cross piece under the front gable after mitering and attaching the 1/4-round. The signs are also cut from lath scrap, glued and tacked into place.

**Step Six** Cut a crescent moon from the 4" x 6" plywood, paint it white, then glue and tack it to the back gable. Install the two eyescrews on the roof ridge, unless you prefer to post mount this house. Drill a 1/4" hole 1" below the entry hole. Cut a 2-1/4" length of dowel and glue it into place.

**Step Seven** The remaining 3/4" dowel is used to attach the miniature birdhouse, which is an optional feature. It is cut from 1/16" stock and glued on. The entry hole is drilled into the block, with a nail for the perch.

# New England Town Hall

Here's a taste of colonial Americana at its finest. This architectural relic of early democracy could host a variety of species—even partitioned as a house for martins. And as with the old town meetings, you are free to interpret the consensus of this design.

## Materials List

|   |   |
|---|---|
|   | *1 x 12 x 22" Pine base* |
|   | *1 x 12 x 20" Pine ceiling panel* |
| 2 | *1 x 12 x 16" Pine walls* |
| 2 | *1 x 12 x 9-3/4" Pine walls* |
|   | *1 x 8" x 8" Pine* |
| 2 | *1/2" x 9-3/4" x 20-1/4" Plywood roofing* |
| 5 | *1-1/4" x 11-1/4" Dowels* |
|   | *1/4" Plywood or solid stock* |
|   | *1/8" Solid stock scrap* |
|   | *2-1/2" x 2-1/2" x 10" Pine* |
|   | *1-5/8" x 1-5/8" x 6-1/2" Pine* |
| 4 | *1/2" Wooden beads* |
|   | *Roof shingles* |
|   | *Bell* |

**Step One** First, cut the base, the four walls and ceiling panel from 1 x pine. The ceiling panel should be cut with a 45° bevel on both long sides to fit the roof panels. Use a jigsaw to cut all the door and window openings in the wall panels. If you choose to make this a martin house, construct inner partitions from 1/4" plywood to create between 8–12 cubicles in a bi-level configuration. Cut your doors and windows accordingly. Refer to the chart on pages 14 and 15 to accommodate other species.

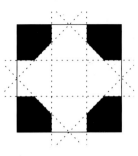

Otherwise, wall up all the openings except one front door with scraps of 1/4" plywood. Then glue and nail this structure together as shown in the exploded view drawing. Let dry.

**Step Two** Cut the 1 x 8" x 8" pine panel diagonally into two right triangles. Then cut both roof panels from 1/2" plywood. The top ridge seam can be miter cut or lapped with a butt joint. The eaves can be cut with a 45° bevel so as not to detract from the bottom tier of shingles. Glue and nail this roof assembly into place, starting with the triangles. Let dry.

**Step Three** Cut eight 1-1/2" squares from the 1/4" plywood or solid stock. Bevel cut the top edges, then use a hole saw to cut 1-1/4" holes through their centers. Insert the four 1-1/4" dowels into these blocks, and glue them into place to form the front portico.

**Step Four** To accommodate the spire, cut two grooves across the roof ridge, toward the front, 2-1/2" apart and to a depth of about 1". Using a coping saw, cut out a 2-1/2" square through the roof panels. Make this opening as snug a fit as possible for the 2-1/2" square spire base.

**Step Five** The spire is the crowning glory, whether you copy this one or free-form your own. This 2-1/2" square base rests on the ceiling panel. The belfry is opened up at the top by making a series of 3" cuts down from the top, then chiseling out the center (see illustration). Cut and chisel the straight angles before the diagonals.

A mitered 1" skirt of 1/4" stock is added just beneath this opening, and capped with beveled and mitered strips of 1/4" stock. Decorative cuts may be added before assembly. The mitered upper fascia is cut from 2" strips of 1/4" stock, including arches cut with a coping saw.

The 1-5/8" square upper spire is bevel cut to a point. Arched panels of 1/4" stock are glued and nailed around the bottom edge, then framed by long rectangular strips of 1/8" stock. 5/8" circles of 1/8" or 1/4" stock can be applied to these. Use a 1-1/4" eyescrew with glue to secure this upper assembly to the center of the 3-7/8" square of 1/4" stock that forms the ceiling plate. A small bell is attached to the eyescrew. Glue and nail all this to the four prongs of the spire base. Mitered 5/8" strips of 1/4" stock form the notched rails. Wooden beads adorn the corners, attached with glue. Dowels can also be used to secure the balls into the rail corners.

This entire structure is firmly secured into the roof assembly with glue. The roof/spire seam should be caulked with waterproof sealant.

**Step Six** All the remaining trim on doors, windows, roof gables, etc. is cut from 1/4" stock to fit, then glued and nailed into place with small brads.

**Step Seven** Cut four 3/4" mitered strips of 1/4" stock to form the front and rear roof edge caps, then glue and nail into place. The shingles can either be purchased ready-made as doll house trim, or cut from solid 1/8" stock. Apply successive beads of silicone across both roof panels, and apply each tier of shingles from the bottom up. Every other row is staggered and filled with half shingles on each end. You can paint the structure traditional white or as you wish to enhance the trim.

148

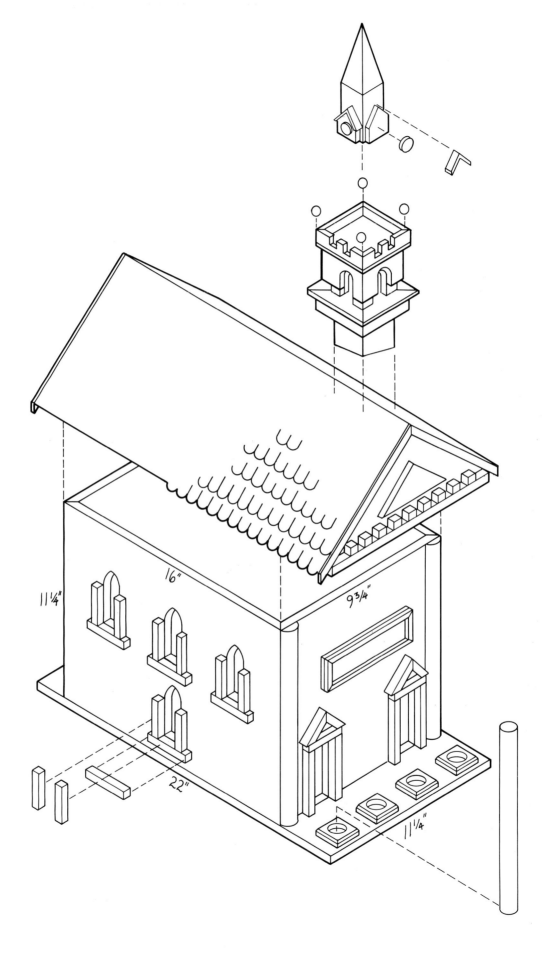

16"

11¼"

9¾"

22"

11¼"

# Grapevine Summer House

This decorative birdhouse, with its husky vines and coiled tendrils, offers breezy shelter for nesting birds. It can be hung under a porch roof or eaves to keep out rain. It can also be built around a gourd for use in colder climates.

## Materials List

*An armful of grapevines*
*A small spool of tie wire*
*Side cutters*

**Step One** Make thin round wreaths and cut all pieces as shown.

**Step Four** Attach E to C as shown.

**Step Two** Start with eight 32" stays and add as many as you desire.

**Step Three** Start with eight 6" roof vines and add as many as you desire.

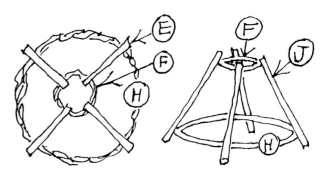

**Step Five** Attach four rafters as shown, then add more.

**Step Six** Bend I into tear drop. Attach ends of E 5" from top of tear drop.

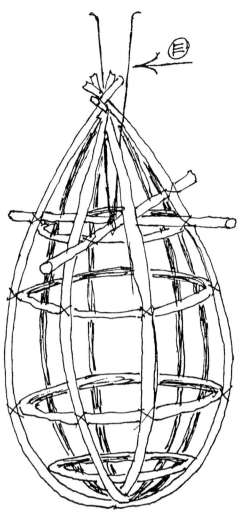

**Step Eight** Attach wire to E for later attachment to top ring.

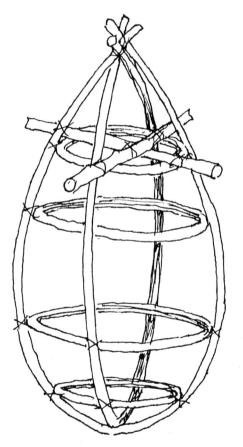

**Step Seven** Add inside rings as shown, then repeat tear drop stays until walls are as full as you desire.

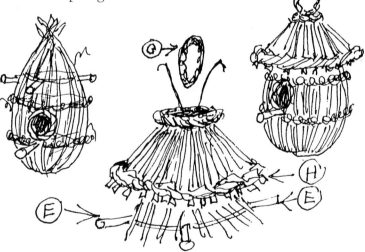

**Step Nine** Wire door and perch in place, then cut out door. Place roof over hanger wires and wire roof H to E. Tie hanger wires to G. Add small vines to outside for decorative trim.

# Feeders

## Mosaic Twig Feeder

Once you get the knack of splitting twigs,
the possibilities for mosaic ornamentation
are endless. This wall-mounted feeder dis-
courages squirrels and mice, yet is easily
refilled to attract all sorts of birds.

# Twig Tent Feeder

## Materials List

|       |                          |
|-------|--------------------------|
|       | 1 x 12 x 12" Pine base   |
| 2     | 1-1/4" dia. x 12" Twigs  |
| 1 or 2| 16" V-shaped twigs       |
|       | 1" dia. x 9" Twig        |
| 3–4   | Coffee cans              |
|       | Bundle of broom corn     |
| 6     | 1-3/4" Wood screws       |
|       | Twine                    |
|       | Glue and assorted nails  |

**Step One** You can saw one V-shaped twig in half, or use two the same size, for the roof frame. They are glued and screwed to the base from the bottom. The 9" twig is glued and screwed between both apexes to form the roof ridge.

**Step Two** Saw the two 12" twigs in half, then glue and nail them around the edge of the base to form a lip for the feed tray.

**Step Three** Open and flatten coffee can barrels, then nail them over the roof frame, overlapping the peak. For a more natural look, tie broom corn over these tin panels with twine. This can be replaced as the birds eat the broom corn seeds. Mount this feeder on a post.

# Mosaic Twig Feeder

## Materials List

|   |                           |
|---|---------------------------|
| 2 | 1 x 12 x 12" Pine         |
|   | 1 x 8" x 10" Pine         |
| 2 | 10" V-shaped twigs        |
|   | 1" dia. x 9" Twig         |
|   | 1-1/4" dia. x 12" Twig    |
|   | 1" dia. x 12" Twig        |
|   | 1-1/4" dia. x 8" Twig     |
|   | 1/4"–3/8" Assorted Twigs  |
|   | Juice can                 |
|   | Large hinge               |
| 2 | 4" Steel L-brackets       |
| 6 | 1-3/4" Wood screws        |
|   | Glue and assorted nails   |

**Step One** The 8" x 10" base and V-shaped uprights are joined in the same manner as the previous feeder. The 9" twig is screwed to the apexes of the uprights. The 8" twig is split in half, then glued and nailed to the side edges of the base. The 1-1/4" x 12" twig is split, and half is attached to the front edge of the base to complete the lip.

**Step Two** The juice can is opened at the top end, then punctured with a can opener around the bottom edge of the cylinder to spill seed. It is screwed to the center of the base. The base assembly is then attached to the bottom edge of one of the 12 x 12" panels with glue and nails. It is reinforced with two L-brackets.

**Step Three** The other half of the 1-1/4" x 12" twig is glued and nailed to the front edge of the roof. The 1" x 12" twig is split for the side edges. Trace a pattern on the roof panel. Split the assorted twigs with a hunting knife and mallet for the mosaic. The smallest twigs may be left whole. Those to be bent can be boiled first. Cut each to the appropriate length, then predrill and nail them into the pattern. The roof will be hinged to the back.

# Bark-Faced Feeder

This classic design has been embellished with a woodsy mix of twigs, mosses and lichens. It is a highly functional feeder that will attract frequent flyers, and it's easy to make.

## Materials List

|   | |
|---|---|
| | *1 x 5" x 7" Pine base* |
| | *6-1/2" x 10-1/2" Bark-faced slab* |
| 2 | *1-1/4" dia. x 5" Twigs* |
| 2 | *2" x 11" Bark-faced slabs* |
| 2 | *2" x 5" Bark-faced slabs* |
| 4 | *#10 Wood screws* |
| | *Eyescrew* |
| | *Glues and assorted nails* |

**Step One** Glue and nail the two 2" x 5" slabs to the 5" edges of the base, flush at bottom. Glue and nail the two 2" x 11" slabs to the long edges of the base, completing the feed tray.

**Step Two** Glue the two 5" posts to each end of the base, reinforcing with screws from the underside. Glue and top screw the roof slab to the posts. Install the eyescrew top center.

**Step Three** Attach all the woodsy ornamentation with clear silicone sealant.

# Thatched Twig Feeder

Here's yet another variation using all natural materials. This post-mounted feeding pavilion features a thatched roof with ornamental wattle railings and sub-roofing.

## Materials List

|   | |
|---|---|
| | *8" x 16" Log slab* |
| 4 | *1/2" dia. x 12" Forked branches* |
| | *Lots of assorted twigs* |
| 3 | *1" dia. x 17" Twigs* |
| | *Bundle of straw* |
| | *Tie wire* |
| | *Glue* |

**Step One** Trim 1" of bark off the non-forked end of each post branch. Drill slanted 1/2" holes for these four corner posts into the log slab, about 5" and 10" apart. Glue the posts into place, rotating the forked tops to accept the roof frame.

**Step Two** Attach four main twig members to the forked post tops with tie wire. The smaller end members should be V-shaped to form a roof peak. Attach smaller V-shaped cross pieces to the longer side members with tie wire. Weave the smaller twigs lengthwise through these cross pieces to form a peaked roof frame.

**Step Three** Insert 3/8" dia. x 10-1/2" twigs into pre-drilled and glued holes in the corner posts for two pairs of top and bottom rails. Wire on a few upright slats, then weave smaller twigs through these to form wattled railings. The upright slats could also be pre-drilled and glued into the railings.

**Step Four** The thatched straw is wired to the wattled roof frame. Lacquer it thoroughly for longer life. Split the 17" twigs that will be wired through the thatch to the frame to form the roof ridge and eaves caps. Add whatever ornamental bracing and decoration you like with more twigs.

# Bird Cage Feeder

Grapevines are a wonderful material to make this charming cage, complete with trapeze. See how many pretty birds try out the swing, swoop down for a tempting morsel, then fly the coop, evading jailbird captivity.

## Materials List

*An armful of grapevines*
*A small spool of tie wire*
*8" dia. Plastic tray (potted
    plant saucer)*
*Side cutters*

*In place of grapevines, you can use
willow or other flexible material.
Tie wire can be found at most any
lumber yard or hardware store.*

**Step One** Roll grapevines into circles A, B, C and F as shown.

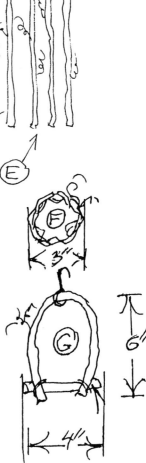

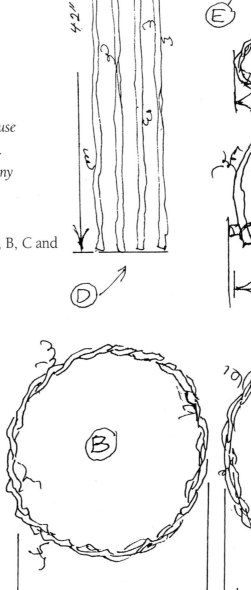

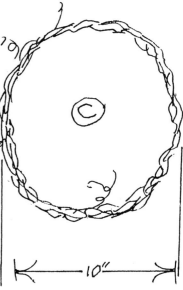

158

**Step Two** Wire four bottom bars E with tie wire to C.

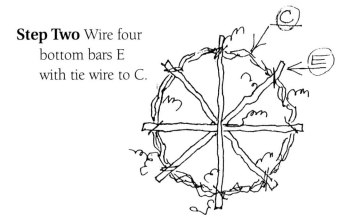

**Step Three** Wire 42" D bars to *inside* of C at joints of C and E. Install only 2 D bars as shown.

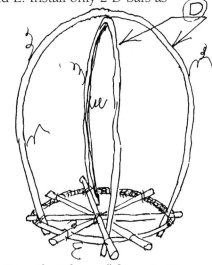

**Step Four** Place B inside D bars 4" from C. Cage bottom wire in place, then insert A 11" from bottom and wire in place.

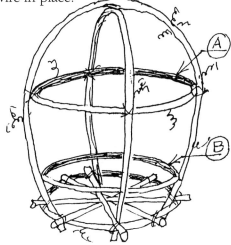

**Step Five** Wrap extra small vines around bottom C and, if desired, around B and A as shown in photo. Place plastic tray in bottom for seed.

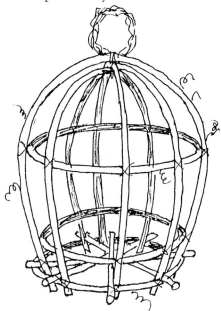

**Step Six** Install last two D bars just as first two were installed. Wire F circle to top, and hang swing inside center.

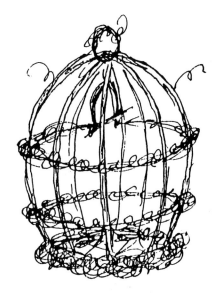

# Traditional Slant

Here's a new slant on a classic birdfeeder design, fashioned out of durable cedar. It's fun to make, and features a clever lift-off roof panel for easy feed loading.

## Materials List

2   *1 x 7-1/4" x 18-1/4" Cedar*
2   *1 x 7-1/4" x 17-1/2" Cedar*
   *1 x 7-1/4" x 5-3/4" Cedar*
3   *1 x 2-1/2" x 4-1/4" Cedar*
   *1 x 2" x 4-1/4" Cedar*
2   *1 x 1" x 5-3/4" Cedar*
2   *1/2" x 1-3/4" x 10-1/8" Cedar*
2   *5/16" x 6-1/8" Dowels*
2   *3-1/4" x 4-5/8" Plexiglass*
   *4" x 9-1/4" Copper flashing*
2   *Rubber bumper knobs*
   *Glue and assorted nails*

**Step One** Cut a 45° bevel on each upper corner of the 1/2" cedar pieces. Drill a 5/16" hole, 1/4" deep, below each bevel. Insert the dowels with glue as you glue and nail the 1/2" stock, centered and flush at the bottom, to the 5-3/4" x 7-1/4" base plate.

**Step Two** Rip cut a 45° bevel on the two 1 x 1" strips. Glue and nail these pieces on the open edges of the base to complete the feeding tray.

**Step Three** Rip cut intersecting 75° bevels on one long edge of two of the three 2-1/2" x 4-1/4" blocks. One of these will be affixed to the removable roof panel. The other supports the two spear-shaped walls, along with the square block opposite, just above the plexiglass slot. Rip cut 45° bevels on the two top long edges of the 2" x 4-1/4" base block.

**Step Four** Cut the two spear-shaped walls from the 17-1/2" lengths of cedar. Cut a 1/4" deep groove in both lower slanted edges of each wall. Glue and nail the walls to the two side blocks and base block as shown in the drawing. Attach the rubber knobs to the base bevels, then insert the plexiglass. This assembly can now be inserted into the center of the feeding tray, and glued and nailed in place.

**Step Five** Rip cut a 15° bevel off one short edge of each 18-1/4" roof panel to intersect as a peak. Place both panels in position, remove the fixed side, then mark the position of the upper beveled block to be attached to the removable panel. Glue and nail the block in place.

**Step Six** Put both panels back in position, and glue and nail the fixed side. Bend the copper in half lengthwise, then lay it over the roof peak. Bend, clip and crimp the ends, then nail them to the removable panel.

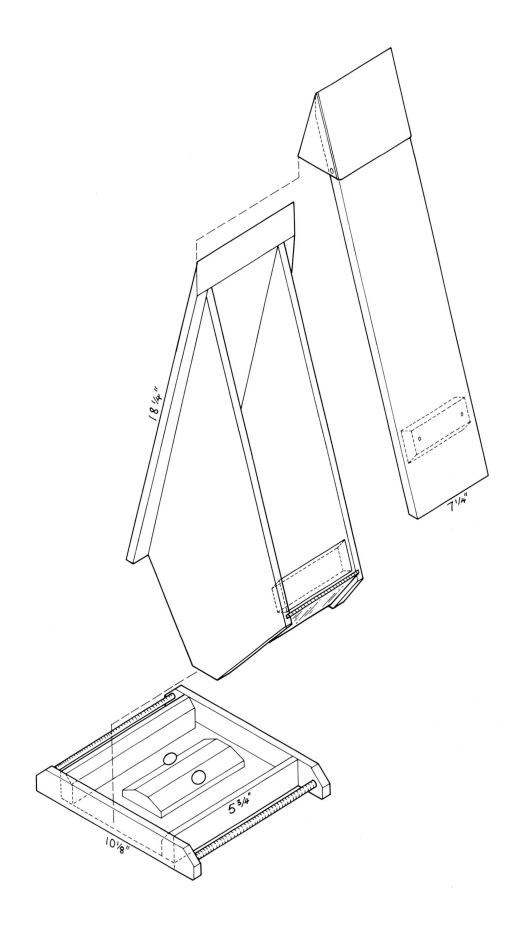

18 1/4"

7 1/4"

5 3/4"

10 1/8"

# Pyramid Canopy

So elegant and simple, this redwood and copper feeder needs no glue or fasteners. The brass chain does all the work. Just hang it, fill it, and watch the birds feed.

## Materials List

| 3 | 1 x 9-1/2" x 11-1/4" Redwood |
|---|---|
| | 12" x 13" Copper flashing |
| 2 | 1/2" Split key rings |
| 5 | 7/8" Brass S hooks |
| 6 | 5/8" Brass S hooks |
| 6 | Brass eyescrews |
| 3 | 8-1/2" Brass chains |
| 3 | 4" Brass chains |

**Step One** Straight cut the 90° notch 1-3/4" into one long edge of each redwood block. Mark another 90° angle from the center of the opposite long edge. Undercut 35° bevels along each diagonal line. Drill a 1/4" hole in each roof panel centered near the apex. (See Diagram 1.)

**Step Two** Cut a triangle with flanges from the copper flashing. (See Diagram 2.) Fold along the dotted lines to create a triangular tray with double thick rims. Drill 1/16" holes through the double thick upper corners of each rim.

**Step Three** If you wish to glue the roof sections together, do so now. However, the sections will hang neatly in place without glue once the chains are installed.

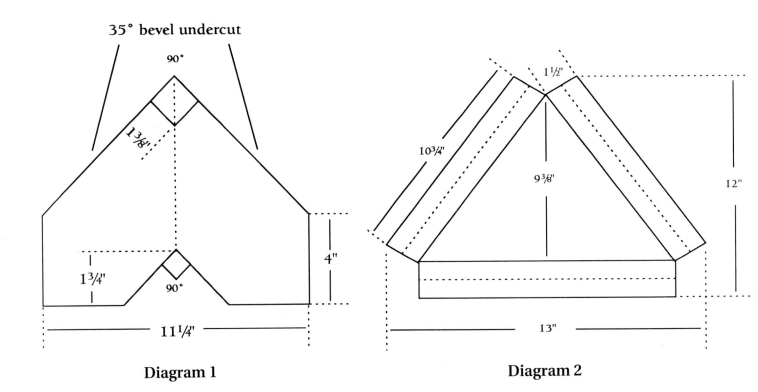

Diagram 1

Diagram 2

**Step Four** On the inside surface of the roof panels, pre-drill and insert eyescrews 5/8" in from each edge of the bottom outside corners. Insert and crimp a 5/8" S hook through each of the six corner holes in the copper tray. Insert and crimp a 7/8" S hook through each of these smaller pairs of S hooks. Open both end links of the 4" chains, hook them on each pair of eyescrews, then crimp them closed. Insert the top of each large S hook through the center link of each chain and crimp it closed.

**Step Five** Join one end of each 8-1/2" chain with a split ring. Pass one chain through each roof hole from the underside. Insert and crimp an S hook through the other end of each chain. Add another S hook to this one. Suspend the structure from this top S hook. Pass a split ring through each chain 1/2" above the apex of the roof, or join them with single chain links (as in the photo).

# Plentiful Pagoda

Three tiers of tempting treats await your famished feathered friends. With an oriental flare, this ingenious design features top-loaded feed that trickles down to fill all levels.

## Materials List

    *3/4" x 17" x 17" Plywood*
    *1/2" x 12-5/16" x 12-5/16" Plywood*
    *1/2" x 7-15/16" x 7-15/16" Plywood*
    *1/2" x 3-13/16" x 3-13/16" Plywood*
*4*   *1/2" x 7" x 13" Plywood*
*4*   *1/2" x 6" x 8-5/8" Plywood*
*4*   *1/2" x 6" x 4-1/2" Plywood*
*4*   *1/4" x 1-1/2" x 17-1/2" Cedar*
*4*   *5/8" x 4-5/8" x 18" Cedar*
*4*   *5/8" x 3-3/8" x 12-1/4" Cedar*
*4*   *5/8" x 3-3/8" x 8-1/4" Cedar*
*4*   *5/8" x 3-5/8" x 4-1/2" Cedar*
    *Glues and assorted finishing nails*

**Step One** In each corner of the 3/4" plywood base, drill a 1/2" drainage hole centered 1" from each edge. Measure 7" from each corner toward the center, and drill four more 1/2" drainage holes. You may wish to cover each hole with a 1" circle of window screen, which you can affix with clear silicone.

**Step Two** Miter cut all the short edges of the 7" x 13" wall panels for corner joints. Rip cut a 37-1/2° bevel along one long edge of each panel for roof joints. Dado cut a 1/2" groove, 3/16" deep, 1" from the top on the non-beveled side. Using a hole saw, cut three equidistant 2" holes centered 1-1/4" up from the bottom edge of each panel. (The holes need to be lower than those pictured.)

**Step Three** Centered 1" from each edge of the 12-5/16" square, drill 1-1/4" holes in each corner, then four more between these. Centered 1" from each edge of the 7-15/16" square, drill 1-1/4" holes in each corner, then a fifth hole in the center. Drill a 3" hole in the center of the 3-13/16" square. Cut the remaining wall panels in the same manner as the bottom tier, with 2" holes centered 1-1/4" from the bottom edge.

**Step Four** Using glue and nails, join the top four wall panels, inserting the 3-13/16" square into the dadoed groove at the top. Let dry, then glue and nail this assembly to the center of the 7-15/16" square. Join the middle tier of walls, inserting the top assembly into the groove. Let dry, then glue and nail this assembly to the center of the next larger square, and so on down to the bottom. Varnish this plywood assembly thoroughly before attaching the cedar roof panels.

**Step Five** Mark a 55° line from each bottom corner of all cedar roof panels to form the trapezoids. The top cap sections will be triangles. Set your table saw blade at 52-1/2°, and cut along each of these lines. Each tier is then glued into place, nailing the top edges into the wall bevels, and angle nailing the bottom corners to reinforce the seams. You can use clear silicone in place of glue for durable roof seams.

**Step Six** You may wish to bevel the 1/4" cedar lath for the tapered look shown here. Miter the corners, then glue and nail each strip to form the lip of the foundation.

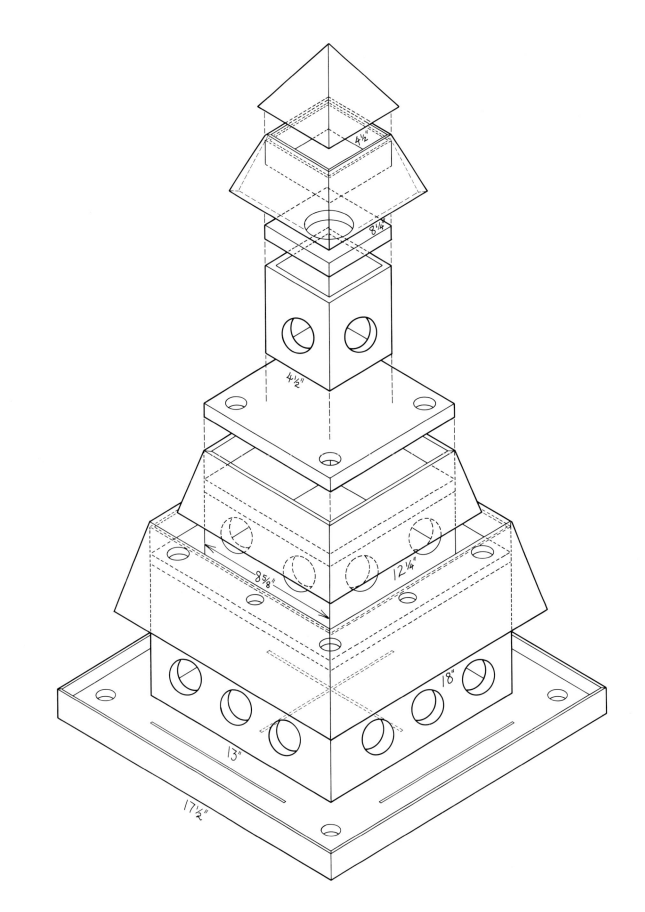

4½"

8¼"

4½"

12¼"

8⅝"

18"

13"

17½"

# English Country Gazebo

This Old World way station for hungry birds has natural appeal as a landscaping ornament. The hexagonal, double-roofed pavilion can be made of cedar, redwood or pine, then left to weather.

## Materials List

2    *1 x 9" x 20" Solid stock*
6    *1 x 5" x 11" Solid stock*
6    *5/8" x 1-1/2" x 9-3/4" Solid stock*
6    *5-1/2" x 11-1/4" x 11-3/4" Triangles of 1/2" solid stock*
6    *4" x 7-1/2" x 7-1/2" Triangles of 1/2" solid stock*
     *3/8" Solid stock scrap*
     *Glue and assorted nails*

**Step One** Lay the two base planks side by side, then trace a hexagon with 9-3/4" sides that fills the area. Cut off the outside corners.

**Step Two** Miter cut both long edges of all six 5" x 11" wall panels at 60° to form the hexagonal chamber. Using a jigsaw, cut the arched window openings in each panel. The bottom sill is centered 2-1/4" from each bottom edge. The openings measure 2-1/4" x 6".

**Step Three** Join the six walls with glue or clear silicone. Use large rubber bands to hold them together while they dry. Small brads can be tapped in to reinforce the seams after the glue is dry.

**Step Four** Apply glue to the bottom rim of the chamber as well as the center seam of the base planks, assemble upside down and top nail the base to the chamber. Then pre-drill and add wood screws for reinforcement. Let dry.

**Step Five** Miter cut the 9-3/4" rail section at 60° Drill 1/2" holes through the center lengthwise for decoration. Glue the adjoining edges, then nail into place. By inverting the structure, you can lay the base over the rails and top nail them. Angled corner nails will reinforce the corner seams.

**Step Six** All twelve roof sections will need to be miter cut at 52-1/2° along intersecting edges to form the hexagonal cones. Join them by applying a large bead of glue or silicone to each seam, then leaning the sections together and pressing them into alignment. Let dry, then sand the seams smooth. The eaves can be trimmed neatly after joining. Each roof section can be glued and nailed into place. You may also wish to add a decorative spire. The stem should be inserted and glued into the apex.

**Step Seven** Cut the six arch-shaped stoops from the 3/8" stock. They should measure 2" x 4". They are simply glued and nailed onto the sills.

**Step Eight** Cut the window trim from solid 3/8" stock. They will measure 3-1/2" x 7-1/2" before cutting. You can gang half or all at the same time depending on whether you use a band saw, a jigsaw or coping saw. Use glue and small brads to secure them in place.

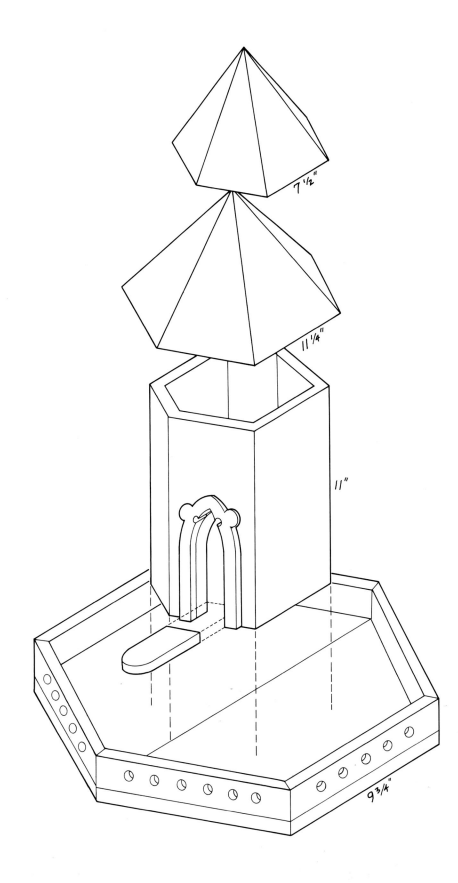

7¹⁄₂"

11¹⁄₄"

11"

9³⁄₄"

# Wishing Well

This nostalgic feeder exudes country charm, and it can be constructed many ways—from a rustic romp to a cooper's dream. No matter, a bird's only wish will be that you keep it well stocked.

## Materials List

|    | |
|----|-----------------------------------|
|    | 1/2" x 6-3/4" dia. Plywood        |
|    | 1/4" x 11-1/4" dia. Plywood       |
| 12 | 1/2" x 2" x 4" Pine               |
| 2  | 3/4" x 3/4" x 11" Pine            |
|    | 1-1/2" x 1-1/2" dia. Dowel        |
|    | 1 x Scrap                         |
|    | 1/4" Scrap                        |
|    | 1/4" x 10" Dowel                  |
|    | 5-1/2" Metal rod                  |
|    | 8" Nylon string                   |
|    | 1-1/2" dia. Wooden spool          |
|    | 5-1/2" Heavy wire                 |
|    | Large eyescrew                    |
| 2  | #8 Wood screws                    |
|    | 1-1/4" dia. Screen                |
|    | Glue and assorted nails           |

The well shown here is basically a cylindrical bucket with a conical roof. This can be constructed using various materials and techniques. It could also be a square or polygonal shape. The structure could even be purchased ready-made. It's entirely up to you.

**Step One** Find some reasonably tight-grained or furniture grade stock for the bucket slats. The 2" x 4" pieces will need to be bevel cut on the long sides at 30°. Using large rubber bands or a circular clamp, glue these slats together into a cylindrical barrel shape. Let dry.

**Step Two** The bucket shown here was taper cut on a machinist's lathe. All you need to do with your polygon is round off the exterior. You can whittle before sanding if you want it really rounded. Also sand the top and bottom rims.

**Step Three** Cut the floor of the bucket to fit snugly after tracing the interior shape onto the 1/2" plywood. Wedge into the bottom with glue and tack it in place. Cut a 3/8" hole in the center, then glue or tack the screen over it for drainage.

**Step Four** The two 3/4" support posts are glued to the sides, nailed at the bottom, and screwed from the inside bucket rim. You may want to notch them as in the photo. If your bucket is tapered, the top should be beveled slightly to join with the roof disk. Drill a 1/4" hole halfway into one post, 1-1/2" from the top, before joining. Glue and nail the roof disk to the posts.

**Step Five** Taper the 1-1/2" dowel at the top before gluing it to the center of the 11-1/4" plywood disk. Cut triangles from the 1 x and 1/4" scrap. Glue the 1 x triangles like spokes around the tapered dowel (see photo). Layer the triangular 1/4" shingles over this substructure with glue. Let dry, then insert the eyescrew at the apex.

**Step Six** Cut the 10" dowel into a 9-1/4" shaft and a 3/4" handle. Drill holes into one end of each to accommodate the metal rod. Bend the rod into a crankshaft, then glue it into both dowels. Drill a 1/4" hole through the undrilled post, 1-1/2" from the top, then insert the shaft. You may glue it in place, or leave it free to turn.

**Step Seven** The bucket shown here was lathe-turned. You can make a reasonable facsimile from a wooden spool, or purchase one from a hobby store in the doll house department. The 5-1/2" wire handle is bent and inserted into pre-drilled holes. Tie the nylon string to the shaft, wrap it, then dangle it to tie onto the bucket handle. Stain the assembly to your taste.

# Covered Bridge

These quaint country crossings may be disappearing from rural landscapes, but they're due for a revival in bird feeder architecture. This perfectly adapted design will experience heavy traffic from birds on the wing, and built out of cedar, may last as long as its predecessor.

## Materials List

| | |
|---|---|
| 2 | 1 x 7-5/8" x 27" Cedar |
| | 1 x 7" x 24" Cedar |
| 2 | 1 x 7" x 8-5/8" Cedar |
| 2 | 1 x 2-1/2" x 8-1/2" Cedar |
| | 1 x 4" x 4" Cedar |
| | 1-1/2" x 1-1/2" x 6' Cedar post |
| 4 | 1/2" x 1/2" x 22-5/8" Cedar |
| 2 | 1/2" x 1/2" x 5" Cedar |
| 28 | 1/4" x 1-1/2" Dowels |
| | Cedar shake shingles |
| 4 | #10 Wood screws |
| 8 | #8 Wood screws |
| | Glues and assorted nails |

**Step One** Rip cut 45° tapered bevels on all long edges of the two 27" roof panels. Cut the 45° roof peak and rounded arch out of both 7" x 8-5/8" blocks at once. Mark the arch with a compass.

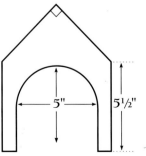

**Step Two** Drill fourteen 1/4" holes along one face of each 22-5/8" rail. They should match up on 1-1/2" centers and be 1/4" deep. Rub glue around each dowel tip before tapping it into the bottom rails. Rub glue on the upper tips before tapping the top rails onto them. Let dry.

**Step Three** Glue and nail the rails to the arch blocks to form the walls. They should be flush at the bottom and at the corners. Let dry.

**Step Four** Glue this assembly to the 24" base, clamping or weighting for tight seams. After seams are dry, reinforce the arches with four #8 screws from the underside corners. Glue and nail the 5" lip molding inside the arch thresholds.

**Step Five** Using clear silicone sealant, glue both roof panels atop the arches. After seams are dry, reinforce the roof to arch seams by top nailing. The shingles are attached one row at a time from the bottom, also using silicone. If you use non-cedar shingles, such as available for doll houses, you should add two coats of polyurethane to protect them.

**Step Six** Cut both scalloped braces from the 2-1/2" x 8-1/2" pieces at the same time on a band saw or jigsaw. Cut a decorative bevel on the edges of the 4" square post block.

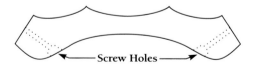

**Step Seven** Attach the post block, bevels down, to one end of the post with two #8 screws. Attach the block to the center of the base with two #8 screws. Attach both scalloped braces to base and post with countersunk #10 screws.

# Cascading Post

This modern design sports multi-level feeding decks that Frank Lloyd Wright might have engineered. The top-loaded feed spirals down around the post, and it's all under one roof. An intriguing blend of function and aesthetics.

## Materials List

|   | |
|---|---|
| | 3-3/4" x 3-3/4" x 5" *Pine block* |
| 4 | 1/4" x 4" x 16" *Plywood walls* |
| | 1/4" x 3-3/4" x 10-1/8" *Plywood partition* |
| | 1/4" x 14" x 14" *Plywood roof* |
| 2 | 1/4" x 8" x 8" *Plywood decks* |
| 2 | 1/4" x 4" x 6" *Plywood braces* |
| | 1/4" x 2-1/8" x 3-3/4" *Plywood floor* |
| 4 | 1/4" x 7/8" x 8-1/4" *Plywood* |
| 4 | 1/4" x 7/8" x 4-1/4" *Plywood* |
| 2 | 1-1/2" *Threaded posts* |
| 2 | *Matching capped nuts* |
| | *Glues and nails* |

**Step One** It should be noted that this entire structure can be built around a pressure-treated 4 x 4 post, the upper 5" of which would be encased. A squirrel barrier would then be advisable. Also, you are encouraged to substitute solid 1/4" stock in place of plywood if you can find it. This is not crucial so long as you thoroughly caulk, prime and paint the plywood structure to withstand the elements.

**Step Two** If you are not building this around a 4 x 4 post, procure a 1" steel pipe (threaded at the top end), and cut a snug hole in the bottom center of the pine block.

**Step Three** Cut 22-1/2° angles across the tops of the wall panels. In one of these panels, cut a 5/8" x 3" slot, the sill of which is centered 5" up from the straight bottom. In another panel, cut the same slot 11" above the straight bottom edge.

**Step Four** Wood glue and rubber bands (for clamping) will be used to join the walls around the pine block, with successive butt joints. However, as you join these, you must also glue in place the central partition as well as the 2-1/8" x 3-3/4" floor of the upper chamber (see drawing). You may wish to pre-glue the floor and partition assembly. Note that the partition is aligned off-center toward the lower chamber, and rests on the pine block inside the four walls. The walls should be turned so that the bevels alternate, creating two planes for the peaked roof. Sand all surfaces flat and square with a sanding block before joining.

**Step Five** Cut a V-slot 7/8" in from each corner on the long edge of the two 4" x 6" pieces. These K-shaped braces will support the decks. (Rather than joining these separate pieces to the main trunk chamber, you could cut the two non-slotted walls to include this irregular shape intact.)

**Step Six** Cut the 4" x 4" upper decks out of one corner of the two 8" x 8" deck pieces. Cut all eight 7/8" strips that form the lips of the decks. Sand all of these surfaces flat and square.

**Step Seven** Glue one pair of decks at a time. Lay the trunk chamber horizontally each time and add weights to all appropriate members so that all seams dry tightly. Sand the seams of the entire assembly once it has dried.

**Step Eight** Cut the 14" square roof panel diagonally with a 52-1/2° beveled angle. Using

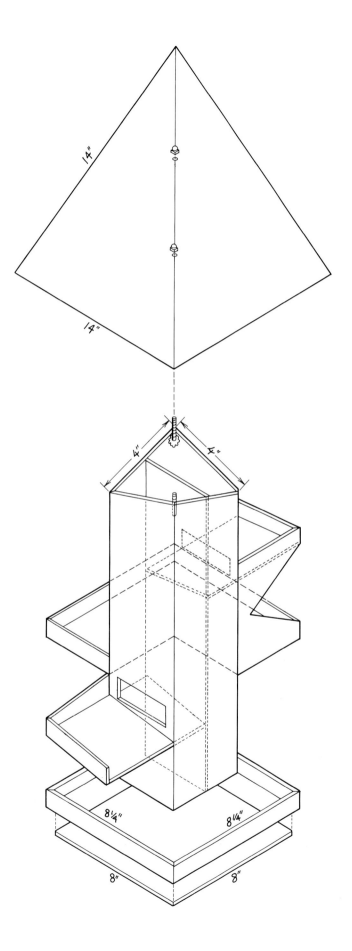

shims to support these angled panels, glue them together along the long beveled seam. (You can glue a triangular block into the center if you wish to brace them.)

**Step Nine** Epoxy the two threaded posts inside the opposite high corners of the trunk chamber. They should extend 1/2" above the corner rim.

**Step Ten** Lay the roof over the center of the trunk chamber. Carefully mark the points where the threaded posts meet the underside ridge. Drill snug holes to accommodate the posts.

**Step Eleven** Thoroughly caulk, prime and paint the structure according to your own taste.

179

# Birdie Can-teen

A child can make this simple feeder with hand tools and minimal supervision. And in addition, it is a very functional feeder that can be decorated many different ways.

## Materials List

|   |   |
|---|---|
|   | *1 x 11-1/4" x 11-1/4" Pine* |
|   | *1 x 7-7/8" x 7-7/8" Pine* |
| 4 | *1/4" x 1-1/2" x 8-3/16" Lath* |
|   | *3-7/8" Dia. coffee can* |
|   | *16' Clothes line* |
| 2 | *#6 Wood screws* |
|   | *Glue and assorted nails* |

**Step One** The pine squares can be cut with a hand saw. Find the center point in both pine squares. Mark two points in each, 3" apart in the center and parallel with each other, and drill 1/4" holes in all four points.

**Step Two** The lath can be glued and nailed in successive butt joints around the base, flush with the bottom, or mitered from 8-7/8" lengths if you prefer.

**Step Three** Cut four openings in one end of the can with a can opener, hammering back the triangular flap with a screwdriver and hammer flush with the can's bottom. The top should be removed.

**Step Four** Paint the can and both plates as you wish. Let dry. Screw the can to the center of the bottom plate from the top, punching holes in the can with a nail and hammer near the perimeter of the circle.

**Step Five** Run the clothes line (preferably plastic coated, to defy squirrel traction) in a long U shape through the top, into the can and through a bottom hole, back up through the other bottom hole and through the top. This can be hung from a big tree or other high places.

# Bird Feeder

This bird likes nothing better than to hang around and feed her fellow fowls. They will visit often to perch on her wings and sample the fruit or bread scraps *du jour*.

## Materials List

|   | |
|---|---|
|   | *1 x 3-1/4" x 9-1/2" Pine* |
| 2 | *3/8" x 2-3/4" x 8" Pine* |
|   | *3/8" x 2-3/4" x 3-1/2" Pine* |
| 3 | *1-1/2" Nails* |
|   | *Eyescrew* |
|   | *Glue* |

**Step One** With a coping, jig or band saw, cut the outlines of the body, wings and tail as shown in the photos, or as you prefer. Whittle the edges into pleasing tapers, except where the wings and tail will join the body.

**Step Two** On a table or band saw, cut a 3/8" notch into the body's tail about 1" deep. With a coping or jig saw, cut a 3/8" x 1-1/2" slot through the belly area. Whittle and sand these junctures until all pieces fit snugly. Glue them in place and let dry. Whittle and sand the tail joint.

**Step Three** Prime and paint the bird as you wish with outdoor paint. This bird has an antique finish. Keep in mind that you may want to wash the bird periodically.

**Step Four** Using a same size nail, drill holes into the top of the body as shown in the photo. Snip the heads off three nails and glue them into these holes with epoxy. Install the eyescrew wherever the piece will balance with food spiked on it.

# Cardinal Dispensation

They say that gluttony is a cardinal sin. See how often you have to refill this tempting see-through feeder, and you may discern which is nobler: man or bird.

## Materials List

| 2 | 2 x 9" x 10" Pine |
| | 1 x 4-1/2" x 4-1/2" Pine |
| 4 | 1/4" x 1-1/2" x 4-5/8" Lath |
| 2 | 4-1/2" x 5-3/8" Plexiglass |
| | Sink stopper |
| | Eyescrew |
| | Glue and assorted nails |
| | Clear silicone sealant |

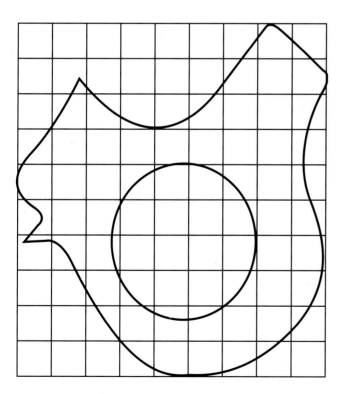

**Step One** Trace a bird pattern on one of the 2 x pine blocks. Cut it out with a jig or band saw. If you have access to a hole saw, cut a 4-1/4" circle out of the center. Otherwise, trace and cut the circle with a jig or band saw. The bottom of the circle should be 1-3/4" from the bottom edge of the bird.

**Step Two** Lay this cut piece on top of the other 2 x pine block, then trace the circle and the outline. Cut this block to match. Glue and clamp them together. Let dry, then sand the seams smooth.

**Step Three** Lay a plexiglass rectangle over one of the holes, leaving a 3/8" opening for seed spill. Trace a C-shaped outline around the hole that has a 5/8" margin. Cut this shape gently with a fine tooth coping saw. Trace and cut the other pane the same.

**Step Four** Cut the 1 x pine square diagonally into two triangles. Miter cut the short edges of the lath, then glue and nail them to the short sides of both triangles, flush with the bottoms. Glue and nail these wings to the body, with the top surface flush with the circle bottoms. Let dry.

**Step Five** Using a hole saw or coping saw, cut a hole in the top of the bird through to the feed chamber, big enough to accept the sink stopper snugly.

**Step Six** Paint the entire assembly to taste. Topcoat with a sealant to preserve the center glue seam.

**Step Seven** Pre-drill the nail holes through the plexiglass. Run a bead of silicone around the curved edges, then nail them into place. Install the eyescrew.

# Catfish Windvane

Reminiscent of primitive American folk art, this whimsical windvane features a unique advantage in bird feeding comfort. No matter which way the wind is blowing, the cat's head always shelters our dainty diners from the elements.

## Materials List

        1 x 12 x 28" Pine
    2   1 x 5-1/2" x 6-1/2" Pine
        1 x 7-1/2" x 8-1/4" Pine
        1 x 5-1/2" x 8-1/4" Pine
        1 x 4-1/4" x 4-1/4" Pine
        1/4" dia. x 1-1/2" x 8" Lath
        5' Heavy wire
    2   2" Lag screws
        16d Nail
        1-1/4" dia. x 6'–8' Post
        Glue and assorted nails

**Step One** First, build the head. Cut 80° bevels around the 4-1/4" x 4-1/4" face block to join with the flared sides. The face surface will then measure about 4" square.

**Step Two** Mark points on both 5-1/2" x 6-1/2" side blocks, 1-1/4" in from each corner on the same long edge. Draw lines from these points to the opposite corners, then cut along these lines at 90°. Bevel the 4" edge at 80° on both blocks.

**Step Three** Mark points on the 5-1/2" x 8-1/4" bottom block, 1-3/8" in from each corner on the same long edge. Draw lines from these points to the opposite corners, then cut along these lines at 90°. Trace this shape onto the 7-1/2" x 8-1/4" top block, with the 5-1/2" edge flush with one 7-1/2" edge. Trace and cut at 90°. Bevel the 5-1/2" edges of both blocks at 80°. (The overhang on the top block is a rain-shed.)

**Step Four** Glue and nail the head together. Let dry, then sand all the seams. Using a coping or jigsaw, cut wavy lines along the outer edges of the top and sides to suggest tufts of fur.

**Step Five** Using a jig or band saw, cut a fish body outline from the 28" board. Save the scrap. A tapered neck area should extend about 4". The bottom edge of the neck must be flat to join with the head, and angled parallel to ground level. A hole, slightly larger than the 16d nail should be drilled about 2" deep, perpendicular to the bottom neck edge. This will keep the feed tray level.

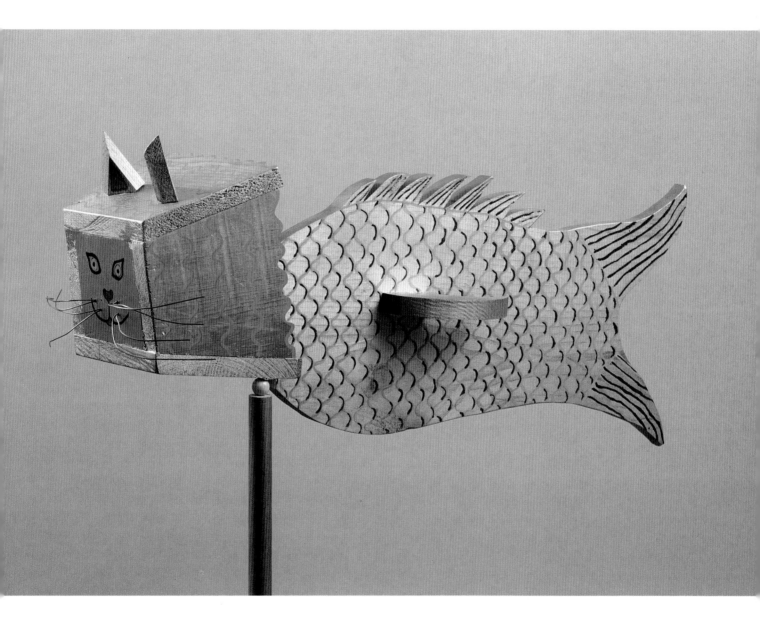

**Step Six** Cut curved side fins from the scrap, then glue and nail them to the body. Bevel cut two triangles to make ears about 2-1/2" tall. Glue and nail them on.

**Step Seven** Glue and nail the neck into the head. Reinforce this joint with two 2" lag screws from the underside of the head. Cut the lath into two 4" lengths. Glue and tack these to the bottom edge of the head, forming a lip for the feed chamber.

**Step Eight** Prime and paint for exterior use to your taste. Cut the wire into four 15" lengths. Bend these in half, then insert into small whisker holes drilled into the face.

**Step Nine** Hack saw the head off the 16d nail after hammering it halfway into the post.

# Window Box

If you've ever wished that birds would come right to your window to feed, now you can sneak a peek through the tulips. Refill the feed simply by raising your window and opening the flower bed lid.

## Materials List

    *1 x 11-1/4" x 14" Pine*
    *1 x 7-1/2" x 21-5/8" Pine*
    *1 x 6-3/4" x 21-5/8" Pine*
    *1 x 5" x 23-1/2" Pine*
2   *1 x 4" x 8-1/2" Pine*
2   *1 x 7/8" x 7-3/8" Pine*
    *1 x 7/8" x 14" Pine*
2   *1/4" x 1-1/2" x 24" Lath*
2   *1/4" x 1-1/2" x 5-3/8" Lath*
9   *1 x 4" x 4-1/2" Pine*
9   *5/16" x 4-1/4"–7-1/4" Dowels*
2   *2-1/2" Hinges*
    *Glue and assorted nails*

**Step One** Mark a point 3-13/16" from each end of the 6-3/4" x 21-5/8" side piece on the long bottom edge. Draw and cut a line from each of these points to the upper corners. Cut a long notch 1/2" x 10-1/2" centered into the bottom edge, or cut 2 or 3 notches (as in the photo). Lay this piece on top of the 7-1/2" x 21-5/8" side piece, trace the diagonal edges to the bottom corners, then 3/4" lines perpendicular to the bottom edge. Cut along these lines. Cut a 60° bevel on one short edge of each 4" x 8-1/2" side piece.

**Step Two** Glue and nail the notched side to the two 4" sides, with the bottom (notched) edge flush with the 4" beveled edges. Join the other big side opposite to form the window box, then join it to one long edge of the 11-1/4" x 14" tray base.

**Step Three** Lay the 5" x 23-1/2" lid on top and mark the screw holes and outline of the hinges. Chisel the hinge area out of the lid edge to recess them flush. Clip 1/8" off each corner for drainage. Install the lid with hinges.

**Step Four** Miter the corner edges of all the lath, then glue and tack them around the lid edge flush with the bottom. Miter the four edges of the 1 x 7/8" strips where they join, then glue and nail them to the tray edge.

**Step Five** Cut each flower and leaf piece from one of the 4" x 4-1/2" block. Drill 5/16" holes into the lid, the flower bottoms and through the leaf centers. Join them with glue. Paint to your taste.

**Step Six** This feeder can be attached with steel brackets on top of your window sill (as shown), or lower so that the flower bed is flush with the sill.

# Breakfast Tray

Start their day off right with a bountiful banquet. This feeder is easy to stock, delightful to watch, and a real treat for almost any of the bird persuasion. What mother wouldn't drop her worm in favor of this early bird special.

## Materials List

|   | |
|---|---|
| | 3/4" x 17" x 23" Plywood |
| 2 | 1/4" x 1-1/2" x 24-1/4" Lath |
| 2 | 1/4" x 1-1/2" x 18" Lath |
| 2 | 1 x 12 x 14" Pine |
| 2 | 1 x 3" x 14" Pine |
| | 1 x 4-7/8" x 11-1/2" Pine |
| 2 | 1" Hinges |
| 4 | #10 Wood screws |
| | Vase |
| | Cup and saucer |
| | Bowl |
| | Flatware |
| | Glue and assorted nails |
| | Epoxy |

**Step One** The only component you must build is the cereal box, but you may prefer to make this oversize tray rather than incorporate a ready-made cafeteria tray. Bevel each edge of the 3/4" plywood at 45°. Cut the bottom corners off each lath strip at 45°. These will butt against each other at each tray corner. Glue and tack the lath to the tray bevels. Drill a 3/16" hole at each corner for drainage. Prime and paint for exterior use.

**Step Two** Cut a 5/8" x 6" slot centered in the bottom edge of one of the 12 x 14" box panels. Glue and nail the 1 x 12's to the 1 x 3" panels to form the box. Let dry, then sand the seams. Prime and paint the box and lid, decorating it as you wish. Epoxy the box to the tray, then reinforce with #10 screws from the underside into the box corners. Install the lid using the two hinges.

**Step Three** All the other table items should be fastened in place with epoxy. For periodic cleaning, use a whisk broom or you can even hose it down.

# Country Storefronts

This replica of quaint village shops might appeal more to you than window shopping birds, but the goods spilling onto the sidewalk are sure to get their attention. Stock each bin with different feeds, and see which birds stop by on their way through town.

Boswell's Feed & Seed

City By-Merchantile

# Country Storefronts

## Materials List

|   | |
|---|---|
| | 1 x 12 x 24-1/2" Pine |
| | 1 x 10" x 24-1/2" Pine |
| 4 | 1 x 6-3/4" x 12-3/4" Pine |
| | 1 x 7" x 24-1/2" Pine |
| | 1 x 2-5/8" x 24-1/2" Pine |
| | 1 x 4-5/8" x 26" Pine |
| | 1 x 7-1/16" x 9" Pine (optional) |
| 4 | 5/8" x 6-1/4" Dowels |
| | 1/4" x 1" x 25" Lath |
| 2 | 1/4" x 1" x 11-3/8" Lath |
| | 1/4" x 15" x 24-1/2" Plywood |
| | 13-1/4" x 24-1/2" Plexiglass |
| | 1/8" Scrap plywood (optional) |
| | 24-1/2" Continuous hinge |
| | Cabinet knob |
| | Glue and assorted nails |

**Step One** Rip cut a 60° bevel along one long edge of the 10" x 24-1/2" piece. To cut the peak in the side and interior walls, the pitch is 30° and centered 4-3/4" from one edge. Cut the 2-5/8" x 24-1/2" strip with 60° bevels on both long edges.

**Step Two** With glue and nails, join the back and four parallel walls onto the 12 x 24-1/2" base, securing them with the narrow top strip across the shorter roof slope. If you wish to add the optional slanted floor baffles, bevel cut the short edges at 45°, then glue and nail them into place.

**Step Three** Cut the roofline and all windows and doors out of the 1/4" plywood sheet. Cut and attach optional trim pieces cut from 1/8" scrap plywood. Paint this panel. Lay the plexiglass sheet beneath this panel, cut semi-circles inside the doorways, then put both in place over the front of the walls. Pre-drill, glue and nail into place.

**Step Four** Cut 60° bevels on both long edges of the 7" x 24-1/2" roof panel. Secure this to the other roof strip with the long hinge. Install the knob near the bottom edge center.

**Step Five** Cut 60° parallel bevels along both long edges of the 4-5/8" x 26" awning panel. Cut the tops of the four dowel support post with a 30° bevel. Glue and nail these pieces into place. Signs cut from 1/8" scrap can be hung with small eyescrews. Tack the lath lip into place, then paint the rest of the assembly.

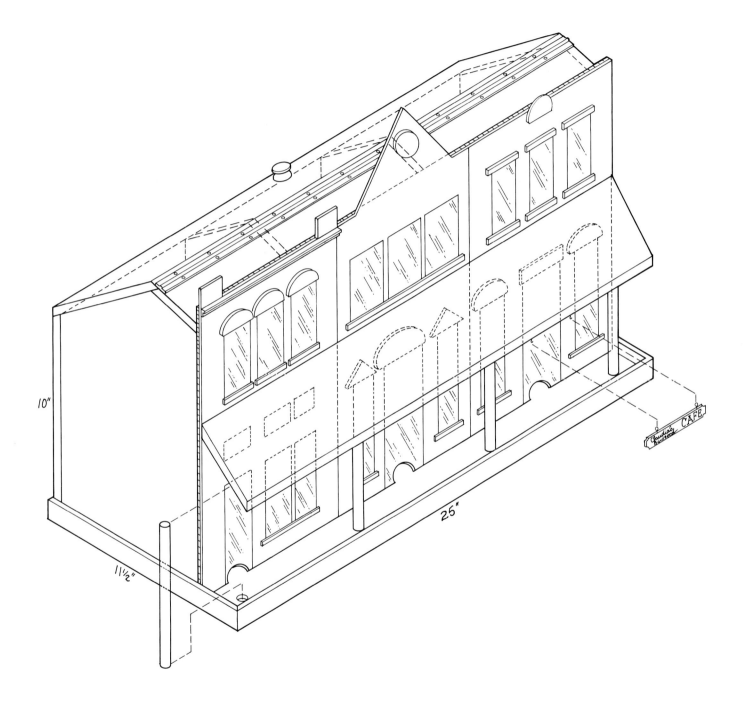

10"

11½"

25"

CAFE

Claudia's
Brebeat

193

# Flying Aces Hangar

After a tough day of aerial acrobatics, your plumed pilots will be happy to taxi down this runway for a snack. A hinged loading door in the rear lets you keep this feeder well stocked.

## Materials List

|   |   |
|---|---|
|   | *1 x 12 x 24" Pine* |
| 2 | *1 x 6 x 12" Pine* |
| 2 | *1 x 8-1/8" x 9-1/4" Pine* |
|   | *1/2" x 12" 1/4-round Molding* |
|   | *12-1/2" x 14-3/4" Aluminum sheeting* |
| 2 | *3" x 4" Aluminum sheeting* |
| 2 | *1" Hinges* |
|   | *Cabinet knob* |
|   | *1/4" x 1" x 4" Lath* |
|   | *1/4" x 5/8" x 5" Lath* |
|   | *1/4" x 1" x 6-1/2" Lath* |
|   | *1/4" x 8-1/2" Dowel* |
|   | *3-1/2" Heavy wire* |
|   | *3" x 3-1/2" Stiff cloth* |
|   | *Toy airplane* |
|   | *Glue and assorted nails* |

**Step One** Cut a 4-1/2" x 5-3/4" front doorway out of one of the 8-1/8" x 9-1/4" wall pieces. Save the cut-out. Draw a line 7/8" above the top doorway edge and parallel to it. Everything above this line will be the arc area. Trace the arc neatly, lay this piece over the other same size piece, then cut the arc in both. Cut a 3-1/2" x 5" hole, centered 4-1/2" up from the bottom edge, in this second wall.

**Step Two** Glue and nail these arc-top walls to the 6 x 12" side walls, butting the side pieces inside the end pieces. Glue and nail the two 1/4-round strips to the top edges of the side walls, rounded faces out and flush with the arc. Let dry. Glue and nail this assembly to one end of the 24" base.

**Step Three** Cut a 3-3/8" x 4-15/16" rectangle from the front door cut-out. Round the top inner edge for clearance. Cut a fan shape out of each 3" x 4" piece of aluminum. Tack a straight edge of each fan to the opposite side edges of the door panel, flush with the outer door surface. Glue and tack the 4" lath strip to the inside top of the door opening to act as a doorjamb. Install the knob, then hinge the door in place.

**Step Four** Tack the aluminum roof sheet into place. If you want extra strength, cut and bend a section of stove pipe instead, and pre-drill the nail holes. Leaving a 1" stem, bend the 3-1/2" wire into a question mark and close the circle. Sharpen the stem to a point with a file.

**Step Five** Cut converging tapers on opposite edges of the cloth. Glue or stitch the funnel-shaped wind sock around the wire hoop. Drill a hole 3/4" into one end of the dowel that is 1/32" wider than the wire stem. Whittle and sand this end of the dowel to round it. Drill a 1/4" hole in the base, then glue the dowel in place. Also glue the airplane in place.

**Step Six** Cut the wings from the 5/8" x 5" lath. Paint them, along with the 1" x 6-1/2" sign. Paint the entire structure to your taste, then glue and tack the wings and sign above the doorway.

**Step Seven** To avoid drainage problems and soggy feed, you can either mount the structure to slope away from the chamber, or add a 1 x 7-3/4" x 12" raised floor before attaching the chamber to the base.

# Intergalactic Snack

To boldly go where no bird feeder has gone before…That is the mission of this stylish seed shuttle. It is a shining tribute to the birds that first inspired man's flight—a spacecraft with real star quality.

## Materials List

1/4" x 16" x 16" *Mahogany plywood*
1/4" x 10" x 14-1/2" *Mahogany plywood*
3   3/8" x 9" *Dowels*
7/8" x 1" *dia. PVC pipe*
*Glues*

**Step One** Cut the base plate from the 16" square plywood, following the diagram. All edges are cut at 90°. Save the scrap.

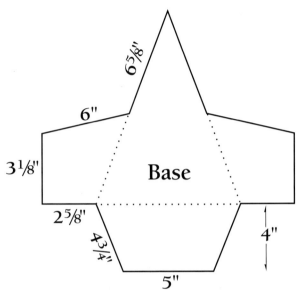

**Step Two** Cut the two sides of the fuselage from the 10" x 14-1/2" plywood with a 42° diagonal cut. Trim these into isosceles triangles with 90° cuts. Bevel the third sides at 48°. Then go back and cut another 3/32" at 42° halfway down each long edge to open up a slot for the top fin.

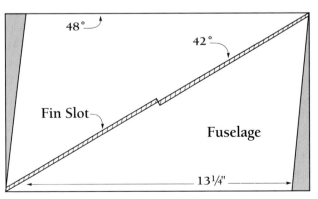

**Step Three** Cut a kite-shaped top fin from plywood scrap. Then cut a 6-1/8" x 4-5/8" x 4-5/8" triangle from scrap. (The dotted line shows the glue seam with the fuselage.) All edges are cut at 90°.

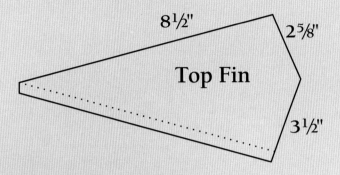

8½"   2⅝"

**Top Fin**

3½"

**Step Four** Run a good bead of glue along every edge to be joined as you assemble the fuselage to the base. Weights can be leaned against the sides and rubber bands clamped around the nose. Let dry, then glue the top fin into the slot, and the triangular baffle into the fuselage.

**Step Five** Cut three 5/8" x 5" strips from plywood scrap. Miter them and glue them to the rear of the base to form a lip for the feed tray.

**Step Six** Cut the PVC in half lengthwise to form two radar dishes. Drill a 3/8" hole in each one. Sharpen the ends of the dowels in a pencil sharpener. Glue the radar dishes onto two of the dowels. Glue the dowels in place with silicone sealant. Caulk all the other seams with silicone after the dowels have dried. Prime and paint for exterior use. This feeder can be hung or post mounted.

# Lighthouse Lunchbox

If you're a coastal dweller, this feeder could be the perfect yard ornament. You may even wish to install a working beacon which will draw extra insect snacks for night birds.

## Materials List

|   |   |
|---|---|
|   | 1 x 6-1/2" x 21" Pine |
| 2 | 3/8" x 3-1/2" x 21" Cedar or redwood |
| 2 | 3/8" x 3" x 10" Cedar or redwood |
|   | 1 x 4" x 14-1/2" Pine |
| 2 | 1/4" x 3" x 14-1/2" Plywood |
| 2 | 3-1/2" x 10" Plexiglass panels |
|   | 3" x 19" PVC pipe |
|   | 4" x 4" x 4" Pine block |
| 3 | 1/4" x 2-1/2" Dowels |
|   | Scrap plastic packaging or bottle caps |
|   | Scrap of window screen |
|   | Shingles |
|   | Glue and assorted nails |
| 4 | #10 Wood screws |

**Step One** Bevel cut both long edges of the 6-1/2" x 21" pine base at 45°. Glue and nail both 3-1/2" x 21" side panels to these beveled edges. Sand both short ends flush, then glue and nail the end panels onto these ends. Trim and sand excess flush with sides after the glue has dried. This tray will hold excess feed, but could also be a wider base with a lath lip.

**Step Two** Cut two 5" blocks from the 1 x 4" pine. Cut two roof-peak tapers at the top of each block. Cut three tapered braces, each 3-1/2" long parallel to the grain, from the remaining 1 x 4" to match the roof-peak angles. Glue and nail the two 1/4" plywood roof panels onto these three braces, spacing them (as shown in the photo) so as to fit either side of the two upright blocks.

**Step Three** You can mill your own shingles from 1/8" stock, or purchase doll house shingles. Apply successive beads of silicone across both roof panels, and apply each layer of shingles, staggering them, from the bottom up.

**Step Four** Cut two 3/8" grooves into each of the upright blocks, stopping 3/4" short of the bottom edge. These will hold the plexiglass. Bevel cut and chisel an indentation on the outside of one block to accommodate the 3" PVC shape. Using a hole saw, cut a 1-1/2" hole through this block and into the PVC while they are standing together. Glue and bolt them together. Cut three 1" holes spiralling up the cylinder for feeding stations. Cut a 1/4" hole 1" below each of these.

**Step Five** Glue the cylinder assembly 3" from one end of the tray, reinforcing with two wood screws up from the bottom and into the block. Attach the other block the same way, inserting the plexiglass in place to determine spacing. Remove the plexiglass, drill two 3/8" drainage holes between the blocks, and glue circles of screen over them. (The photo shows dowel pegs for roof alignment, but these are optional.) Cut a rounded notch in the roof to fit around the cylinder.

**Step Six** This beacon was lathe-turned from a 4" block of wood. Another effective approach would be to join concentric circles of wood with a cross-cut section of a plastic bottle in the middle. The bottom must fit neatly inside the cylinder to act as a stopper.

**Step Seven** After painting the structure, the dowel perches can be glued into place. Sections of curved plastic packaging can be glued under the feeding holes with silicone or epoxy. If you prefer, glue bottle caps into these holes and pack suet into them for the winter months.

# Tropical Island

Birds can snack after bathing in this tropical paradise. Pipe in a little reggae or calypso music, and they may never want to leave.

## Materials List

|   | |
|---|---|
|   | *1 x 12 x 14" Pine* |
|   | *1 x 8-1/2" x 10-1/2" Pine* |
| 2 | *1/2" x 13" Copper pipe* |
| 6 | *1" Styrofoam balls* |
| 6 | *Paper clips* |
|   | *Aluminum sheeting scraps* |
| 2 | *#9 Wood screws* |
|   | *Clear silicone sealant* |

**Step One** Cut an irregular oval out of each pine piece using a coping, jig or band saw. Using a router, sander or hand tools, round off the top edges of these pieces if you want a naturally tapered beach and greenery. Cut a 5" circle out of the center of the smaller piece to cradle the feed. Using a bead of silicone and woodscrews from the underside, join these two pieces.

**Step Two** Bend each copper pipe gently into curved palm trunks. Use tin snips to cut palm fronds out of aluminum sheeting. Leave 3/8" x 1" stems that will be glued into the pipes with silicone. Straighten one end of each paper clip. Insert these straight ends through the styrofoam balls until the looped end is flush. These wire stems will be inserted with the frond stems. Paint the trunks, fronds and coconuts with enamel before gluing them into place with silicone.

**Step Three** Drill two 1/2" holes slanted into the island base. Silicone the trees into place and let dry. Paint the island well with enamel to seal it against the rotting effect of water. You can either float the island or rest it on a brick inside your bird bath.

# Seed for Sail

You'll have more than gulls circling this vessel of victuals, eager to sample the catch of the day. Hang a few mesh bags full of thistle seed over the sides, fill the hold with tasty morsels, then run signal flags up the mast that say "good eats."

## Materials List

|   | |
|---|---|
|   | *1 x 4" x 24" Pine* |
|   | *1 x 2-5/8" x 3-3/4" Pine* |
|   | *1/4" x 1" x 7" Pine* |
|   | *1 x 2" x 4" Pine* |
| 6 | *1/8" x 1-3/4" x 25"–28-1/2" Poplar* |
|   | *1/4" Lath scrap* |
|   | *1/2" x 36" Dowel* |
|   | *1/4" x 17" Dowel* |
| 2 | *1/4" x 13"Dowels* |
|   | *1/4" x 11" Dowel* |
|   | *1/4" x 7" Dowel* |
| 5 | *1/4" x 3-3/4" Dowels* |
| 4 | *Eyescrews* |
|   | *Nylon string* |
|   | *7" x 13" Canvas* |
|   | *Toy bucket, anchor and chain* |
| 3 | *1" dia. Screens* |
|   | *Glue and assorted nails* |

**Step One** Cut the curved hull bottom with an 80° bevel all around. Cut the stern block as shown in the diagram. The 2-7/8" bottom edge should be cut on an 80° bevel. Glue the stern block on top of the hull bottom. Let dry.

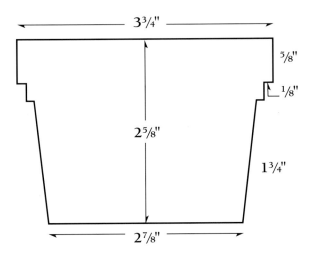

**Step Two** Each end of the 7" bow stem should be cut at parallel 45° angles. Cut one end of two 1-3/4" x 25" strips at 45°, then bevel the insides of these edges slightly to join with the bow stem. Run a good bead of glue on the lower stern, hull bottom edges and lower bow stem. Tack the side strips to the stern, then clamp them to the bow stem, which gets glued to the hull bottom. Let dry.

**Step Three** Sand the bow joint down to a taper before attaching the next side strips. Glue, tack, clamp, and let it dry. Sand the new bow joint before attaching the last strips. After they have dried, sand the bow and trim the top edges flush with the stern block.

**Step Four** Glue the 2" x 4" block, centered 15" from the stern, to the hull bottom. Glue a brace cut from 1/4" scrap over this, resting across the middle side strips. Enclose the bow with two triangular pieces of scrap if you wish.

**Step Five** Drill a 1/2" hole through the center brace and into the block to support the mast. Drill three 1/4" drain holes across the bottom, then glue the screens over top. Drill a 1/4" hole into the bow stem to support the 7" bow sprit. Drill a 1/4" hole at each corner of the stern and both sides of the center brace to support the 3-3/4" posts for the tarp. Glue all these dowels into place.

**Step Six** Drill a 1/4" hole through the mast, 7-1/2" up, for the 17" boom. Drill a 1/4" hole 3" from the mast top for the 3-3/4" yardarm, and another 9-1/2" from the top for the 11" yardarm. Glue these dowels into place. Install an eyescrew next to each tarp support post, then rig the boat with nylon string.

**Step Seven** Glue each long edge of the canvas around a 13" dowel. Let dry, then drape it over the boom. The dowels can either be tied or glued directly onto the tarp posts. Mount this feeder on a post.

# Victorian Gazebo

Nothing quite matches the charm of turn-of-the-century architecture. This feeder could serve as an attractive focal point in a formal garden, at the same time luring colorful creatures to feed.

## Materials List

| | |
|---|---|
| | 1 x 11-1/4" x 11-1/4" Pine |
| | 1 x 10" x 10" Pine |
| 4 | 9" Triangles of 1/2" plywood |
| | 1/4" x 4-1/2" Dowel |
| | 3/8" x 8" Dowel |
| | 1/8" x 5-1/2" Dowel |
| 10 | 5/8" Wooden beads |
| 4 | 3/4" x 3/4" x 5-1/2" Pine posts |
| 4 | 3/4" x 1-1/16" x 1-1/16" Pine blocks |
| 4 | 1/2" x 3/4" x 8" Pine |
| 4 | 1/4 x 1-1/2" x 11-5/8" Lath |
| 3 | 1/4 x 3/4" x 8-1/2" Lath rails |
| 18 | 1/4 x 1/4" x 3" Lath ballisters |
| 8 | 1/4 x 3/4" x 2-3/4" Lath scrolls |
| | Doll house shingles |
| | Aluminum sheet scrap |
| | Clear silicone and assorted nails |

**Step One** Cut and sand the two foundation plates from 1 x 12 pine. Cut a 5" circle out of the center of the smaller plate using a jigsaw, and sand.

**Step Two** Rip cut (from 1 x stock) the four 5-1/2" square posts, then cross-cut each post into a 3" and a 2-1/2" length. Next, rip cut the four 1/2" strips (from 1 x), each measuring 8" long. These will be butt joined to form the top frame that supports the roof. Finally, rip a 5" length of 1 x into a 1-1/16" width, then cut four 1-1/16" blocks to go on top of the posts.

**Step Three** Miter cut four 11-5/8" lengths of lath to form the lip around the base. Next, rip cut three 8-1/2" lengths of lath to a width of 3/4" for the rails. Miter cut all but the two ends which will join the posts at the opening of the feeder. Out of a 13" length of the same lath, rip four 1/4" strips, then a fifth strip from what would have been the fourth 3/4" x 8-1/2" rail. Cut these into eighteen 3" ballisters.

**Step Four** Measure and glue the four 3" sections of corner posts into place, then glue the three rails around the top. Let dry, then wedge and glue the ballisters into place. Let dry. Reinforce the corner posts with a nail or screw from underneath. Then glue and top nail this assembly onto the bottom plate with the two grains running perpendicular. Glue and nail the mitered lath lip around the perimeter. A small drainage hole can be drilled in each corner.

**Step Five** Glue the 1-1/16" blocks onto the 2-1/2" upper post sections. Glue and nail the roof frame together with butt joints. Let dry. Drill 3/8" holes, each 1/2" deep, into the centers of the upper and lower post sections. Cut the 3/8" dowel into four 2" lengths, thread two wooden beads over each one, and join all the post sections with glue. While the glue is wet, align the roof frame over the posts and glue it in place onto the post blocks.

**Step Six** Two of the three sides of each 9" roof triangle can be bevel cut for tighter joinery. Lean these roof panels together, joining them with silicone. Let dry, then glue onto the roof frame.

**Step Seven** Sharpen one end of the 1/4" dowel to a point. Drill perpendicular 1/8" holes through the center of this dowel, then insert two 2-3/4" lengths of 1/8" dowel through the holes. Glue in place. Cut the letters N, E, W and S from

aluminum sheet, and silicone them onto the ends of these small dowels. Glue two beads, pre-drilled with 1/4" holes, onto the main dowel either side of these small dowels.

**Step Eight** Using a coping or band saw, cut the eight scroll pieces from lath. They can be glued into place after they are painted. Drill a 1/4" hole at the apex of the roof. Glue the weather-vane assembly into this hole.

**Step Nine** Apply successive beads of silicone onto two opposite roof panels, and apply each row of shingles from the bottom tier up. Let dry, then trim the diagonal edges with a coping saw from the bottom up. Apply shingles to the other two roof panels, let dry, and trim. Paint the entire piece to your taste. Apply two coats of polyurethane to the roof shingles.

# Castle Keep

This aviary compound features all the amenities: house, rooftop bath and turret feeders, proving that a bird's home is his castle. Fortify your feathered friends in this medieval marvel.

## Materials List

4   *1 x 12 x 10" Pine*
2   *1 x 8-3/8" x 8-3/8" Pine*
4   *1 x 5" x 20" Pine*
4   *1/4 x 1-1/2" x 20-1/2" Lath*
4   *2" x 12" PVC pipe*
    *7-3/8" x 7-3/8" Plastic tray*
8   *1/2" x 1/2" x 8-3/8" Pine*
4   *1 x 3-1/2" Circles of pine*
33  *3/4" x 3/4" x 1-1/4" Pine blocks*
    *3-1/4" x 4-3/4" Pine door*
4   *1/4" x 6-1/4" Dowels*
    *Aluminum sheet scrap*
4   *Small eyescrews*
    *9" Chain*
    *3-1/2" x 4-1/4" Wire mesh*
    *Glue and assorted finishing nails*

**Step One** It should be noted that, depending on the dimensions of the rooftop tray (or baking pan) you find, the size of the castle can be adapted accordingly. So find your bird bath tray first.

**Step Two** Miter cut the 1 x 12 pine to 10" lengths (or to fit other tray) to form the castle walls. Cut square notches in the top edges for battlements. Rip cut eight 8-3/8" pine strips 1/2" square. Miter cut these to recess into the top and bottom of the castle walls. Glue and nail the bottom tier of these, recessed 3/4" from the bottom edge of each wall.

**Step Three** Glue and nail the four wall sections together. Cut the two 8-3/8" square panels from 1 x pine. Glue and nail one of these, recessed 1/2" from the top of the battlement cutouts. Glue and nail the remaining mitered 1/2" square strips above this panel into place.

**Step Four** Cut the 2" PVC pipe into 12" lengths. Cut a 1/2" x 1-1/2" slot in one end of each pipe. Pre-drill and screw, at top and bottom, each pipe to the walls at the front and back corners.

**Step Five** Cut four mitered 5" x 20" planks from 1 x pine to form the blue moat. Glue and nail, from the inside bottom edge of the castle walls, these moat planks into place. Glue and tack the lath lip into place around the perimeter. Finally, insert the 8-3/8" square bottom panel into place, and secure with glue and angled nails.

**Step Six** Cut four 5-pointed asterisk shapes from the 3-1/2" circles of 1 x pine. Also cut four 1-1/2" circles of pine. Rip cut 3/4" strips of 1 x pine, to be cut into 33 blocks of 1-1/4" lengths. Glue five of these onto the tops of each asterisk. Glue and screw the 1-1/2" circles beneath them. Drill 1/4" holes into the top centers to accommodate the dowel flagstaffs.

**Step Seven** Cut the four lengths of 1/4" dowel. Notch one end with a fine coping saw blade. Cut long triangles of aluminum sheet to wedge into place as flags. Glue these flags into place.

**Step Eight** Cut a 3-1/4" x 4-3/4" door from 1 x pine. Round off one end. Glue and nail into place. Glue the remaining nine blocks into place around the doorway. After these are

painted, the wire mesh and eyescrews with chain will be installed. Drill the bird house entry hole above the door.

**Step Nine** Paint as you wish. The mortar lines can be added with a small-tipped paint pencil. The turret tops are removable in order to load seed into the turret towers. Drainage holes can be added to the moat.

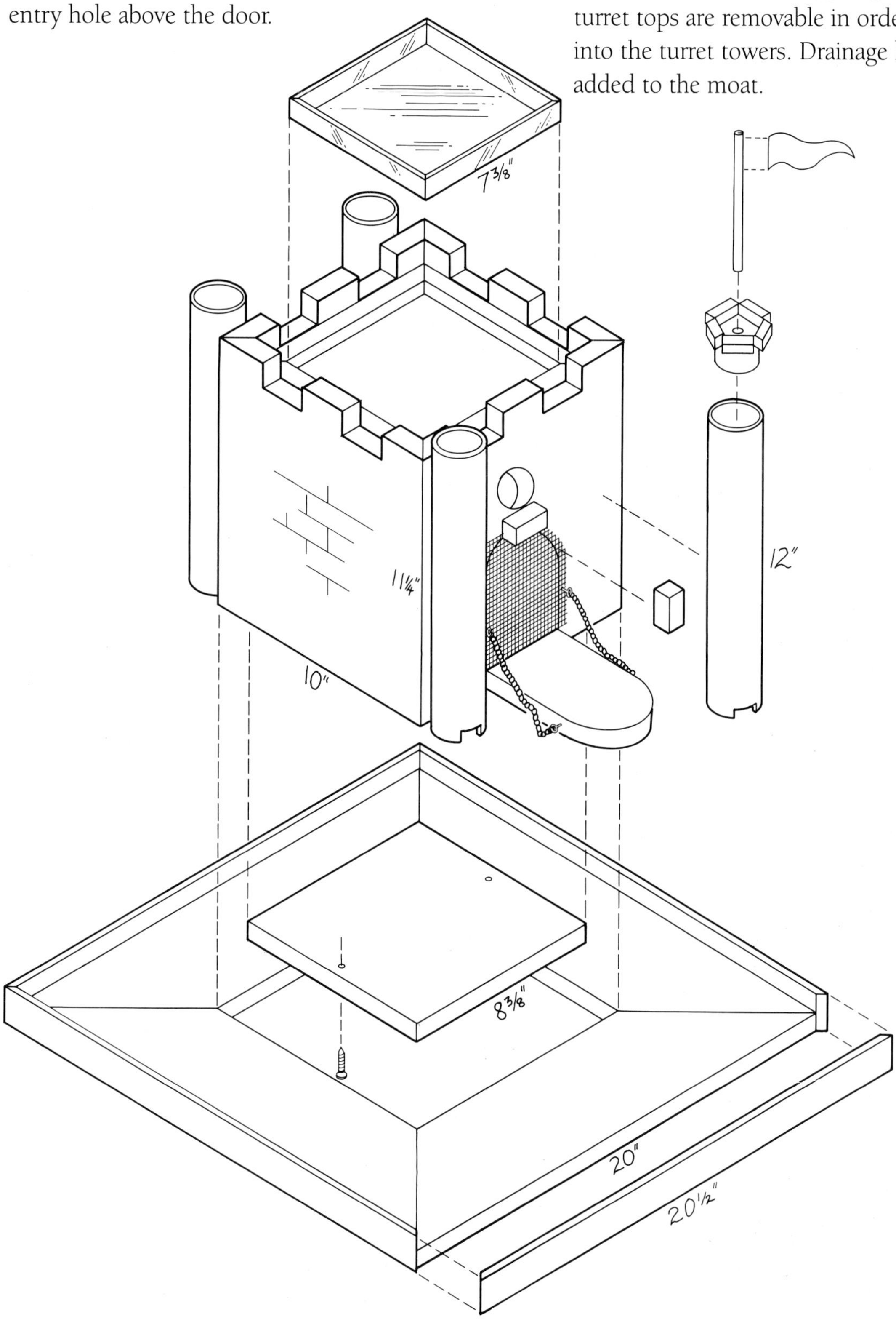

7³/₈"

12"

11¼"

10"

8³/₈"

20"

20½"

# Carousel Cuisine

Fanciful animals orbiting a seed dispenser—how could a hungry bird resist? And what if the saddled species were all sorts of birds? Then again, you may elect to display this spectacular feeder indoors with nuts and candies for our own kind.

## Materials List

| | |
|---|---|
| 2 | 1/2" x 16" x 16" Mahogany plywood |
| 8 | 1/2" x 7" Dowels |
| | 1/2" x 13" Dowel |
| 8 | 3/16" x 7" Dowels |
| | 3/16" x 2" Dowel |
| 8 | 1/4" x 6-5/8" x 9-1/2" x 9-1/2" Plywood triangles |
| 8 | 1/4" x 1-3/8" x 6-3/4" Mahogany plywood |
| 8 | 1/4" x 3/8" x 6-15/16" Mahogany plywood |
| 8 | 1/4" x 3-1/2" x 3-3/4" Mahogany plywood |
| 8 | 4" x 5-1/4" Medium acrylic safety glazing |
| 8 | 1/2" x 1/2" x 6-3/8" Molding |
| | 1-1/4" Wooden bead |
| | 3/8" Wooden bead |
| | Toothpicks |
| | Glue |

**Step One** Cut two identical equilateral octagons from the 16" square plywood. Draw the four intersecting lines from each pair of opposing points on both pieces. Mark 4-3/8" in from each of these points along all eight spokes to determine the centers of the support posts. On one piece, draw four more intersecting lines between the midpoints of each edge. Mark 3" in from each edge along these bisecting spokes to determine the animal mounting posts.

**Step Two** Line up both hexagons, the piece with more lines drawn on top of the other. Drill 1/2" holes through both pieces on the centers marked for support posts. Drill 3/16" holes on the centers marked for animal mounting posts. Drill a 1/2" hole in the very center of one of the hexagons. With a compass, mark a 6" circle in the center of the other hexagon and cut it out with a jigsaw.

**Step Three** Each of the eight support posts must be rip cut with two 1/8" grooves 135° apart. See the diagram to make a jig that will facilitate these two cuts. Fill the lower ends of these grooves with 1-1/4" lengths of toothpicks, glued flush with the bottoms to act as stops for the acrylic panes.

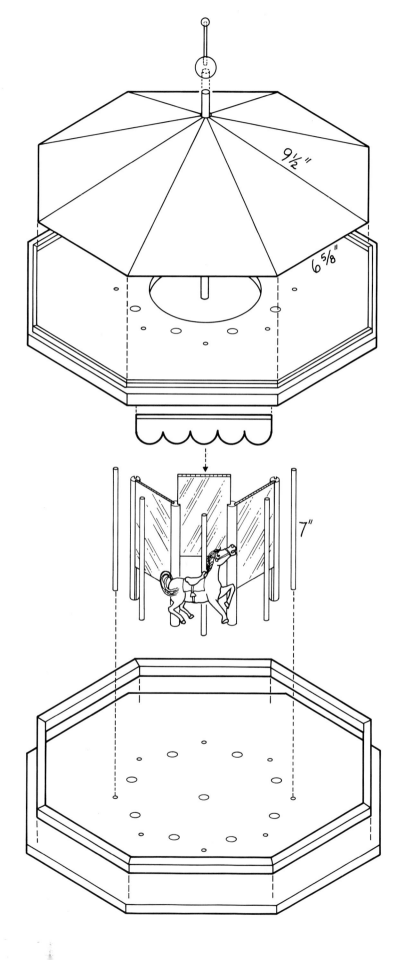

9½"

6⅝"

7"

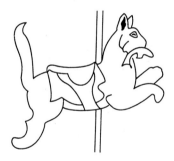

**Step Four** The lip on the lower hexagon can be made with 1/2" stock—square or rounded, half-round or other mouldings. Miter cut the ends at 67-1/2°, then glue them around the perimeter. Cut five rounded scallops into one edge of each 1-3/8" x 6-3/4" piece. Miter cut the ends to 67-1/2° and glue around the outer edge of the other hexagon. (Glue the top edges flush if you plan to install outdoors, since drainage will be a factor.) Miter the 3/8" strips the same way, and glue on as trim.

**Step Five** Paint all dowels and both hexagons, except the 1/2" ends of dowels to be glued, before joining. The acrylic panes can be cut using an inexpensive plastics cutting tool with a straight edge. Glue and tap each dowel into the bottom hexagon. Insert the acrylic panes as you go so as to align the support posts before they dry. You must also insert all dowels into the upper hexagon and tap into place before the glue dries. Let everything dry.

**Step Six** Miter cut one long edge of each roof triangle at 70°. Lay the panels together over tape strips, edge to edge, bevels up. Run a good bead of glue down each seam, fold the panels into a cone and tape the last seam. Let dry, inverted. Drill a 1/2" hole at the apex from the underside. Glue the 1/2" center post into the base. Check the fit of the roof over this post, then trim if necessary and sand all edges and seams.

**Step Seven** Drill a 1/2" hole 3/4 of the way into the larger wooden bead. Drill a 3/16" hole in the top, and into the smaller bead. Glue this assembly together, then onto the apex of the roof. Paint the roof and spire. Pennant may be glued to the spire's shaft.

**Step Eight** Using the patterns, or your own imagination, cut the animals out of 1/4" plywood with a coping or band saw. Paint them as you wish, and glue them to the posts.

## MATERIALS LIST

- (2) 1 x 12 x 22" Western red cedar
- 1 x 12 x 18" Western red cedar
- 1 x 2-1/2" x 19-1/2" Western red cedar
- 1 x 2" x 11-1/4" Western red cedar
- (3) 1 x 2" x 21" Western red cedar
- (2) 1 x 3-1/2" x 14" Western red cedar
- (2) 1 x 2" x 14" Western red cedar
- (12) no.8 x 1-1/4" Brass flathead woodscrews
- Button screw hole plugs
- 8d Galvanized finish nails

**East is East and West is West . . . and what better place for them to meet than in the generous and contemplative art of bird watching? Most birds, after all, are no respecters of national borders; their country is the skies, and their summer and winter homes are commonly nations apart. So bring a little of the Far East into your Western yard, and invite these feathered aeronauts to rest and dine in your pagoda feeder.**

**Purity and simplicity are the key words in this pagoda design, where they're combined to create a surprising elegance. Following those mandates, this feeder takes its grace from minimalism and from the beauty of unfinished cedar stock.**

The Lark

The roof panels are cut from 1 x 12, each being 22" long and beveled to 45° along one long edge. The tray is an 18" length of 1 x 12, surrounded by two 1 x 2-1/2" x 19-1/2" sides, each with a decorative 30° bevel along one edge, and two ends, also cut from 1x stock, measuring 2" x 11-1/4".

The roof and base are connected by an assembly consisting of a ridge pole (1 x 2" x 21", with one long edge double-beveled to a 90° peak); two side supports (each 1 x 2" x 21", with a 45° bevel on one long edge to meet the roof); and two main poles (each 1 x 3-1/2" x 14", with a 3/4" x 2"-deep notch centered in a 90° point on one end to receive the ridge pole. To cut this end, first draw the 45° lines that form the peak with a tri-square. Then set the saw blade to a 2" height and mortise the notch. Finish by following the pencil lines to form a 90° peak with two 45° miters. A pair of cross braces (freehand the curves on one 2" x 14" strip of 1x; then cut it out, trace it onto another board, and cut a second to match) have 1/4"-deep by 3/4" mortises at points 1" in from the ends of the unscrolled edges to receive the roof supports.

To assemble the feeder, hold each tray end in position on the base and scribe a line. Then center the main poles along these lines and secure them with no.8 x 1-1/4" brass flathead wood screws. Now fasten the tray ends to the base with 8d galvanized finish nails. Next, center the ridgepole in the notches in the two uprights and fasten the roof sides to the main post with more 8d nails. With that done, center the side supports in the mortises of the cross braces, and screw them on. Finally, slip that assembly up until it meets the roof and is centered. Then drill and countersink before joining the cross braces to the poles with no.8 x 1-1/4" screws and plugging the countersinks with button plugs. (At this point, you may want to add a few more 8d nails to further secure the roof.)

Enjoy the visitors who seek the solace of your pagoda, and be sure to keep it well supplied all year for those that decide to stay. Many of your guests will, however, refresh themselves and then travel on. Wish them "sayonara" when they go.

The Jack-Daw

## MATERIALS LIST

4 x 4 x 10" Salt-treated
  pine
2 x 10-1/2" x 14" Clear
  all-heart redwood
2 x 10-1/2" x 7" Clear
  all-heart redwood
2 x 2-5/8" x 3-5/8" Clear
  all-heart redwood
2 x 3-1/2" x 4-7/8" Clear
  all-heart redwood
1" x 10-1/2"" x 25-1/4"
  Clear all-heart redwood
(16) no.10 x 2-1/4" Brass
  flathead woodscrews

**During planning and construction, everyone referred to this feeder as "the Frank Lloyd Wright," all the while recognizing that there's really no such thing as a generic Wright building. America's greatest architect never repeated himself, nor was he derivative. Nonetheless, this project shows heavy Wright influence. The overlapped horizontal members are reminiscent of Falling Water, while the angled roof is more characteristic of his Prairie Style. The emphasis of natural materials is a hallmark in most Wright structures, making this one of our favorites.**

This is the sole example in this book where variable mounting is not an option. The 4 x 4 post is an integral part of the structure—just as Mr. Wright would have wanted it. You'll need at least a 10-footer to keep the terrace out of kitty reach once you've buried 18" of the post in the ground, and a predator barrier will be required.

We've also cut loose and splurged on this project: other than the post, which is pressure-treated pine, all the wood is quarter-sawn clear all-heart redwood. Expensive, admittedly, but the visual interplay of the wood's color and grain with the planar design is what makes it work. Feel free to substitute a less-expensive species if you find yourself balking in the checkout line at the lumberyard, but do look for a board with the straightest, most vertical grain possible. Otherwise, warpage is likely.

To simplify the following construction description, let's talk about the feeder from one angle. Imagine that you're looking at it from the side, so that the long deck projects straight out to the left. Start by cutting the top of the post to a 75° angle (the point will be to the right), and then dado two 1-5/8"-deep grooves just shy of 1-1/2" wide across it—one on the right side with its upper edge 3-1/4" from the top, and the other on the left starting 7" down. Decks of 2 x 10-1/2" redwood slide into these dados, with slots cut just wide enough to offer a tight fit without need for pounding.

The lower (left) deck is 14" long and is offset toward you 1", leaving 4" on your side and 3" on the back. The upper deck measures 7" and is offset just the opposite—3" on your side, 4" in back. A 3-5/8" isosceles right triangle cut from 2x stock and screwed to the deck and the post supports the upper deck, while a 4-7/8" isosceles right triangle supports the lower one.

Our feeder's roof is a 1" x 10-1/2" x 25-1/4" piece of redwood. This thickness would normally be called four quarters (4/4) and may not be readily available in your locale. In that case, a 1x board (about 3/4" thick) would make a suitable substitute. The roof rests on the top of the post with 6" projecting to the right of the post and a 1" offset to the front (to be directly above the larger deck). Don't fasten this board to the post yet.

Two columns help support the roof, both cut 5" long from 2 x 4 redwood, with a 75° angle on one end. Position these boards an inch in from the edge of the deck and slide them away (or toward) the post so that the roof fits flush to their tops and that of the post. Now secure the roof and columns to the deck and post with brass screws.

Redwood is exceedingly durable, so preservatives really aren't necessary for this feeder. If you're very fond of the unweathered redwood color, a clear, water-repellant coating would be acceptable. Otherwise, the wood should be left to change with its environment—in process with its clientele.

# A Seedy Eatery

**Back in the days before the golden arches, small, family-owned roadside diners dotted the landscape, offering culinary adventure (and even risk!) to the traveler or vacationer. You can still find a few of these gems, of course, serving (depending upon their location) fried chicken, barbecue, fish and chips, or the ubiquitous burgers and hot dogs. We're afraid that dining dangerously in places like Joe's is an endangered pastime. So, in tribute to the perfect pieces of pie (as well as the horrible cases of heartburn) of the past, we've designed this blue-highway beanery to cater to the weary travelers along your local migration route.**

All of the major components are cut from 1x lumber. The roof front measures 9" x 10", and its back 4-5/8" x 10", both beveled to 40° along one edge to meet at the peak. Two false walls fit inside the roof—each measuring 3" x 5" with one end mitered to form an 80° peak—to allow it to be securely slipped atop the walls without fasteners.

The diner's right and left sides measure 6-3/8" x 9", and are each mitered to the same 80° peak used on the roof supports. The front, which rides up allowing seed to spill beneath its lower edge, is a 6-3/8" x 9" board, beveled to 40° at one end to match the slope of the roof. The back, also beveled to the roof's pitch along one long side, measures 7-1/4" x 8-1/8".

An interior ramp funnels seed down into the dining area. It measures 5" x 8-1/8" and is beveled to 45° at each long end. The floor of the diner, which overlaps the base and will actually receive the seed, is an 8-1/8" x 8-1/8" square. Its dining area is enclosed by a railing consisting of two 1-1/2" x 2-1/2" side walls and a 1-1/2" x 9-1/2" front piece. The pillars, which will be glued into the front corners of the railing, are each 1 x 3/4" x 5-1/2", beveled to 40° at the top to support the front of the roof.

And how about a pair of outdoor tables for fair-weather fowl? Simply cut two discs from 1/4" plywood, using a 2-1/2" hole saw. Bore 1/4"-diameter holes, centered and 1/8" deep in each, and matching 1/4"-deep holes in the appropriate positions on the base. Then glue 2" lengths of 1/4" dowel in each disc, and glue the assemblies into the base.

Attach the interior supports to the roof with glue and 6d galvanized finish nails. Then do the same with the base/diner unit, gluing the seed ramp down after the walls, base, and floor are together. Remember, the roof should simply slip onto the walls, so it can be removed to add seed as needed.

The paint scheme is, of course, up to you. We suggest, though, that you take to the byways (or to the back roads of your memory) and pick out a particular ptomaine palace to commemorate. And don't expect big tips from your customers, they're likely to be cheep and ask that the meals be put on their bills.

## MATERIALS LIST

1 x 9" x 10" Pine
1 x 4-5/8" x 9" Pine
(2) 1 x 3" x 5" Pine
(3) 1 x 6-3/8" x 9" Pine
1 x 7-1/4" x 8-1/8" Pine
1 x 5" x 8-1/8" Pine
1 x 8-1/8" x 8-1/8" Pine
(2) 1 x 1-1/2" x 2-1/2" Pine
1 x 1-1/2" x 9-1/2" Pine
1 x 3/4" x 9-1/2" Pine
(2) 1/4" x 2-1/2"-diameter Plywood
(2) 1/4" x 2" Dowels
6d Galvanized finish nails

The Buzzard

# The Gazebo

**Designed to complement our Southern Mansion bird house, the gazebo bird feeder is fairly simple to construct but quite dramatic visually. It also happens to be a case where our anthropomorphic indulgence works out particularly well for the birds.**

## MATERIALS LIST

1/2" x 9" x 2' OSB
1/2" x 5-3/4" x 9" Plywood
3/4" x 10-1/8" x 10-1/8"
    Plywood
3/4" x 11-1/2" x 11-1/2"
    Plywood
Chair caning
1/4" x 1/2" x 5' Pine
Assorted doll house porch
    posts
Body putty
Fiberglass roving
6d Galvanized finish nails

The hexagonally peaked roof is, in appearance at least, the most imposing component of the structure. But, thanks to the use of a few construction short cuts, it needn't give you nightmares. Begin with a 2' (or slightly longer) piece of 9"-wide 1/2" oriented strand board (or 1/2" plywood.) Set your miter gauge to 22-1/2°, and cut a right triangle off one end. Now flop the board, and make another 22-1/2° cut to produce an isosceles triangle with a base of 7-1/2" and a height of 9". Go on, flopping and turning the wood as necessary, to produce five more identical triangles.

Here's the short cut: Normally, each of these would have to be beveled if they were to fit together to create a roof. We've avoided that problem by joining the square-cut panels with body putty reinforced with fiberglass roving. Happily, the putty has a gray color when it sets that resembles a slate roof. (Another tip: You might want to make a hexagonal collar of scrap wood to hold the roof in "peak" form while it dries.)

The arched walls incorporate a trick of their own. Each is simply a 1/2" x 5-3/4" x 9" plank with its long edges bevel-cut to 30°. Then a 4"-diameter hole saw is used to bore an opening 3-3/4", on center, from one end. Straight cuts tangent to the hole and parallel to the sides proceeding to the base complete the archway.

The hexagonal floor, cut from 3/4" plywood, measures 5-1/2" on a side and 10-1/8" across. The base, upon which the floor sits, is another 3/4" plywood hexagon, but with 6-1/2" sides, that measures 11-1/2" across. It's probably best to draw these first, then set your miter gauge to 30°, and cut along the markings.

The walls, floor, and base can be assembled with construction adhesive and sparing use of 6d galvanized finish nails. Once the basic structure is together, you might want to add some ornamentation. To form railings, we cut out pieces of chair caning and glued them into a sandwich of 1/4" X 1/2" wood rails. On top, we whittled and sanded a combination of turned doll house porch posts and a wooden bead to form a spire.

Painting this feeder, except for the chair caning, is better left to last. We chose a simple white to match our Southern Mansion bird house, and left the slate-toned body putty as is. The roof is probably heavy enough to stay put if simply set in place, but it can be secured with two 2" lengths of plumber's perforated pipe-hanging strap, secured to the walls and the underside of the roof with brass flathead wood screws, if you want the extra protection against strong winds.

Fill it with the appropriate seed, and you might get to see goldfinches grazing in a gazebo. Gee.

The Magpie

221

# A Plywood Parthenon

Modeled after one of the first, great Doric temples, our Parthenon bird feeder draws its beauty from the classic simplicity of its lines. And, while it's not exactly a beginner's level woodworking project, you'll find that many of its components are disarmingly easy to shape and assemble. Just approach the job with the proper attitude. And, to paraphrase Pallas Athena, Greek goddess of wisdom and patroness of the original Parthenon, always "measure twice and saw once."

To begin, cut the base and ceiling from 3/4" plywood; the former will measure 15-1/2" x 21-1/2", the latter 14-1/2" x 20-1/2" with an access hole cut in its center with a 6" hole saw. Now cut the 1x stock that will eventually form the upper and lower sockets for the columns. You'll need four strips measuring 2" x 21" and four more of 2" x 15".

The next step is a bit tricky. Your aim will be to shape 1-1/2" square pillar pedestals along these strips. To do so, first set your table saw for a depth of 1/4" and crosscut multiple dadoes, removing 1-1/2" to leave 1-1/2" blocks at 1-1/2" intervals along the strips. Next, rip the edge of each piece of stock with your rip fence set to remove 1/4" in width and the blade height set to remove 1/4" in depth. The result will be a series of 1/4"-high blocks. each 1-1/2" square, spaced evenly along the lengths of stock.

With that done, take a break from the tricky stuff by cutting 20 columns from 1" dowel, each measuring 7-1/2" long.

The roof assembly is next. Its base is a 15-1/2" x 21-1/2" sheet of 1/4" tempered hardboard. When this is cut, center it on the 3/4"-plywood ceiling, clamp it in position, and bore four evenly spaced 1/2" diameter holes, each 3/4" deep, to accept the dowel plugs that will hold the roof in place. (If you like, you can glue the 1" long dowel segments into the ceiling at this time . . . the roof base will slip over them later.)

The roof panels consist of two 21-1/2" x 9-1/4" sheets of 1/4" tempered hardboard. When you make your long cuts, tilt the table saw blade to about 18° and rip one long edge on each piece, then spin them around and rip the remaining long sides to produce the beveled, parallel edges that will form the roof peak and the eaves.

*Marginal Material*

*In this and a few other projects in this book, we've used tempered hardboard for structural elements. Sharp-eyed readers will note that it was not recommended in the chapter on materials. Truth be told, we'd like to have used something more durable, but plywood, which is thicker, would have looked wrong. Tempered hardboard is rated for moist applications, but we still encourage you to keep it well protected with paint.*

## MATERIALS LIST

3/4" x 14-1/2" x 20-1/2"
    Plywood
3/4" x 15-1/2" x 21-1/2"
    Plywood
(2) 3/4" x 4" x 20" Plywood
(4) 1 x 2" x 15" Pine
(4) 1 X 2" x 21" Pine
(20) 1" x 7-1/2" Dowels
(4) 1/2" x 1" Dowels
1/4" x 15-1/2" x 21-1/2"
    Tempered hardboard
(2) 1/4" x 9-1/4" x 21-1/2"
    Tempered hardboard
6d Galvanized nails

The roof gables are cut from 3/4" plywood. To shape them, start with two pieces, each about 20" long by about 4" wide. Lay one piece on your table saw, and adjust it so that the saw blade will form an 18° rip cut. Then tack a piece of rectangular scrap to the close end so that scrap will slide against the rip fence maintaining the 18° angle. (Be sure to hammer your nails into the scrap at a location where the blade will miss them.) Run the gable through the saw, then use the waste from that cut to serve as a guide to form the second cut that completes the peak. Repeat to shape the rear gable. (This sounds more difficult than it is, but you might want to experiment on some scrap lumber before you cut the good stuff!)

The Long-Eared Owl

Now miter the ends of the upper and lower pedestal strips to produce two equal-sized picture frames, with those raised blocks that are halved by the miter cuts meeting at each joint to form new pedestals. Fasten these frames, centered, to the base and roof with glue and 6d galvanized nails. Then, using a pencil and a straight edge, mark diagonals on each raised pedestal to determine the center point, and drill 1"-diameter holes, to a depth of 1/4", into the center of each one. (If you've got a drill press, it'll make this job easier.) With that done, change bits and drill one 3/8" hole in each corner of the base, just inside the pedestal frame, for drainage.

Now you can glue the roof assembly together, taking special care to get a good seal at the peak. (We didn't use any hardware here, but 6d galvanized nails, run through the roof and into the 3/4" plywood gables, would certainly help hold everything more securely.)

When the roof assembly has dried thoroughly, you'll probably want to paint all of the components before fitting them together. A flat white latex is a good choice and is really all that's needed to produce a striking feeder. You might, however, want to go the extra mile and use a fine brush and gray paint to flute the pillars and add some fanciful heroic carvings on the gable ends as we did. Then, just slip the Parthenon together. It's really quite sturdy as is, though you might want to use glue on the column tops and bottoms to be safe. (Don't, however, glue the ceiling dowels into the roof. You'll need access to the 6" hole to fill and clean the feeder.)

Admittedly, our Parthenon feeder isn't a single afternoon's project, but it'll amply reward the time you spend building it. After all, you simply have to add some millet and sunflower seeds and you'll have a veritable Greek chorus in your own backyard!

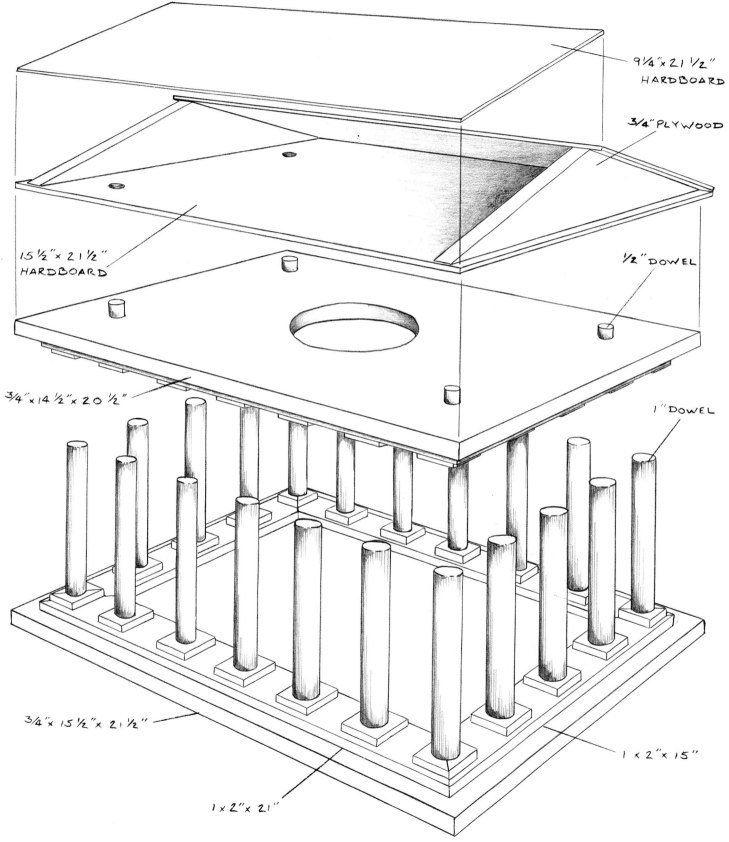

9¼"x 21½"
HARDBOARD

¾" PLYWOOD

15½"x 21½"
HARDBOARD

½" DOWEL

¾"x14½"x 20½"

1" DOWEL

¾"x 15½"x 21½"

1 x 2"x 15"

1 x 2"x 21"

225

# Baths

## Materials List

*An armful of grapevines*
*A small spool of tie wire*
*8" dia. Plastic basin (potted plant saucer)*
*Side cutters*

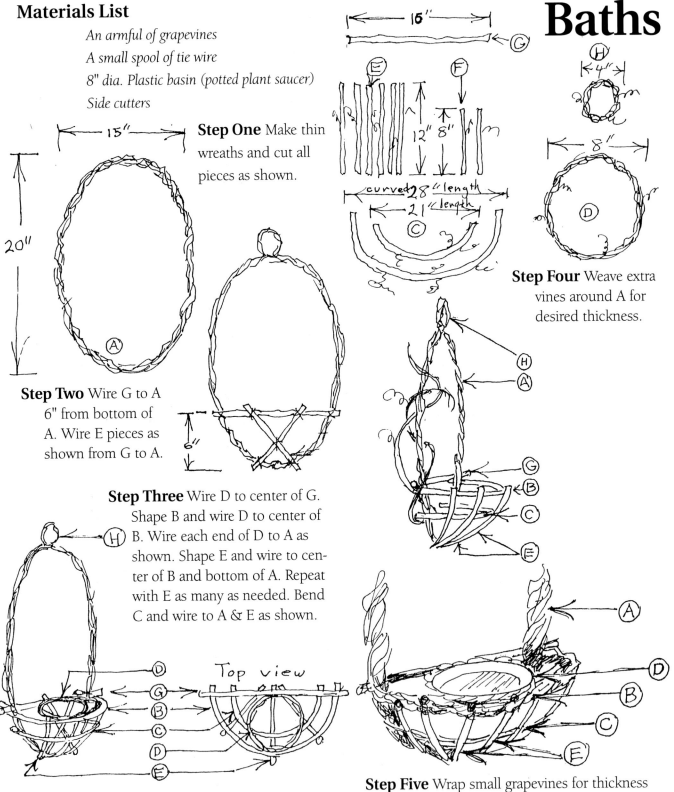

**Step One** Make thin wreaths and cut all pieces as shown.

**Step Two** Wire G to A 6" from bottom of A. Wire E pieces as shown from G to A.

**Step Three** Wire D to center of G. Shape B and wire D to center of B. Wire each end of D to A as shown. Shape E and wire to center of B and bottom of A. Repeat with E as many as needed. Bend C and wire to A & E as shown.

Top view

**Step Four** Weave extra vines around A for desired thickness.

**Step Five** Wrap small grapevines for thickness desired and attach H to top of A. Use 8" clay or plastic flower pot tray for bath basin.

# Wall Hanging Bath

Not all bird baths sit on pedestals. This woven basket cradles a basin and belongs on a vine-covered wall next to a garden. It could also be used as a feeder.

# Swimming Pool

Even birds need a recreational splash now and then. And what fun you'll have watching them do back flips and belly flops off the high dive. Sprinkle some seed around the patio furniture, and watch them frolic.

## Materials List

|   | |
|---|---|
|   | 1/2" x 12" x 24" Plywood |
|   | 3/4" or 1" x 12" x 24" Plywood |
| 2 | 1/4" x 1-1/2" x 24-1/2" Lath |
| 2 | 1/4" x 1-1/2" x 12-1/2" Lath |
|   | 1/4" x 1-1/2" x 6" Lath |
|   | 3/4" x 3/4" x 1-3/8" Pine |
|   | 3/32" x 46" Brass rod |
|   | 1/16" x 40" Brass wire |
|   | 3-3/4" dia. Dome from plastic bottle |
|   | 3/4" x 1" dia. Dowel |
|   | 5/16" Wooden bead |
| 2 | 7/8" x 3-1/4" Grosgrain ribbon |
|   | Polyurethane (can be water base) |
| 7 | #9 Wood screws |
|   | Glue and brads |

**Step One** Use a jigsaw to cut a kidney-shaped hole through the 3/4" plywood to form the pool basin. Then, using a coping saw, cut a taper into each side of the 1-3/8" pine block to form the pedestal for the table. Glue the sanded pedestal onto the deck, reinforcing it with a wood screw from underneath. Glue the deck onto the 1/2" plywood base, reinforcing it with the six remaining screws from underneath.

**Step Two** Miter the edges of the four long lath strips to fit around the base and deck. Glue and tack the lath around the edges. Cut the 6" lath piece into the following: (2) 5/8" x 3-1/2" diving boards, 3/4" x 1-1/16" lifeguard seat, 5/8" x 5/8" step, and a 1-1/2" dia. circle. Drill a 3/32" hole through the center of this circle, another into the pedestal, another through the 3/4" section of dowel, and another into the wooden bead. Glue the dowel into the top of the dome. Let dry. Using glue in all joints and seams, assemble the patio table with a 4" length of brass rod.

**Step Three** All the furniture is soldered together using brass rod for the ladders and vertical supports, with brass wire for the chairs, hand rails, and seat back. They are painted silver after assembly. The high dive and lifeguard chair stand 3-1/8" tall. The low dive is 3/8" above the deck. The chair back frames are 2-1/2" long and 1-1/8" wide. The chair seat frames are 2" long. Each piece of furniture is glued into 3/8" deep holes in the deck. The ribbon is glued or sewn to the chair frames. After painting everything, coat the basin with 2–3 coats of polyurethane.

# Drive-Thru Bird Wash

Falcons and Thunderbirds have been zipping through these automated tunnels of suds for years now, emerging clean and glistening. Isn't it time to offer this dandy device to all the dirty birds in your neighborhood?

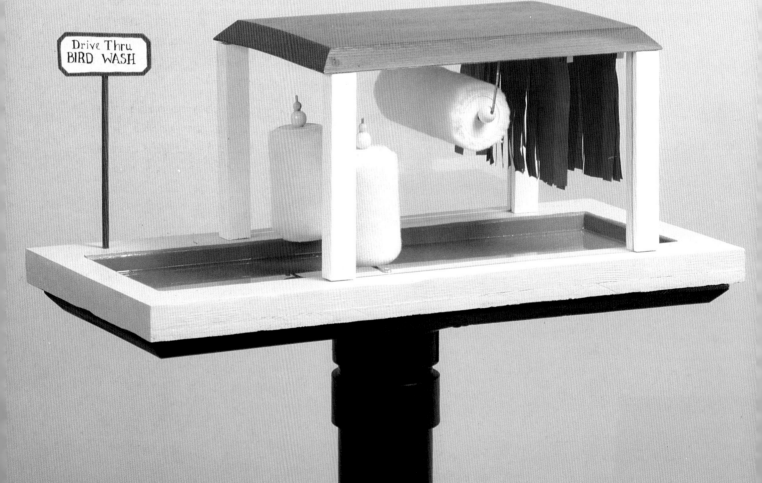

## Materials List

|   | |
|---|---|
| | 1 x 10-7/8" x 24" Pine |
| | 1/2" x 10-7/8" x 24" Plywood |
| | 1 x 9" x 13-3/4" Pine |
| 4 | 3/4" x 1" x 7" Pine |
| 2 | 7" x 11-3/4" Plexiglass |
| 2 | 1/4" x 3/8" x 7-1/4" Pine |
| 2 | 4-3/4" x 7-1/4" Rip-stop nylon |
| | 6-1/4" Paint roller |
| 2 | 4" Paint rollers |
| 6 | 3/4" x 1-15/32" dia. Pine disks |
| | 3/32" x 14-1/4" Brass rod |
| 2 | 3/32" x 7" Brass rods |
| 4 | 5/8" Wooden balls |
| 2 | 5/16" Wooden balls |
| | 1/4" x 8" Dowel |
| 4 | 1/4" x 1-3/4" Dowels |
| | 1/8" x 1-1/2" x 3-3/8" Lath |
| 8 | #8 Wood screws |
| | Glue and assorted nails |
| | Small wire staples |
| | Polyurethane (can be water base) |

**Step One** Cut a 6-1/2" x 21" hole in the center of the 24" pine. Rip cut a 1/4" deep groove down one 3/4" face of each 7" pine post to accept the plexiglass. Cut a 45° bevel on all four edges of the pine roof block.

**Step Two** Drill a 3/32" hole through the center of each pine disk. If you can't find a dowel that fits snugly into the paint roller, cut the disks from 1 x stock with a hole saw. Glue the disks into the rollers flush with the ends.

**Step Three** Bend the 14-1/4" rod into a tall C-shaped rectangle, the long back of which will be tacked to the ceiling with staples. The long side measures 7-1/4". The bracket bends 90° down to 2-1/4", leaving 1-1/4" on each end to bend 90° through the wooden bead and into the disk. Bend both shorter rods into L-shapes, the long stem of which measures 5-1/4". Bend the shorter ends into tight eyelets to accept the mounting screws. Slip the rollers onto the stems, and glue the wooden beads on top.

**Step Four** Cut 4" slits into the nylon to make fringe. Tack these strips to the 1/4" x 3/8" x 7-1/4" pine, then glue and tack them to the ceiling 1-1/4" and 3-1/2" from one edge. Tack staples over the roller support rod 6-1/2" from the same edge. Screw the two upright rollers 3/8" from the edges of the basin, and 10" from one end of the 24" pine.

**Step Five** Drill a 1/4" hole 1" into the center of one end of each 7" pine post. Drill four 1/4" holes through the 24" pine that form a 8-3/16" x 12-3/8" rectangle. The holes closest to the rollers should be 2-1/8" away from the roller mounting screws.

**Step Six** Glue a 1-3/4" dowel into each post. Fit the plexiglass into the post grooves, then glue the posts to the base, tapping the dowels into place. Glue and top nail the roof on to the posts. Let dry.

**Step Seven** Glue the 24" pine base to the 1/2" plywood foundation, reinforcing with the six remaining screws from underneath. Flatten one side of the top inch of the 8" dowel, then glue it to the lath sign. Drill a 1/4" hole in the base, and glue the sign in place.

**Step Eight** You may want to paint as you assemble, or paint everything after assembly. After painting, apply 2–3 coats of polyurethane to the basin.

# Credits

## Projects designed and constructed by:

Ron Anderson: 176, 196, 210

J. Bishop: 56, top right

Lee Berry: 68, 72, 75, 76, 78, 80, 87, 218

Odell Brookshire: 64

Don Daniels: 150, 158, 226

Mark Dockery: 136, 140, 144, 155, 172, 181, 198, 202

Mike Durkin: 180, 182, 184, 188, 200, 204, 207

Garden Source, Atlanta GA: 52, 67

Harold Hall: 60, 61

Bobby Hansson: 50, 134, 153, 154

Michael Hester: 174

D. Holmes: 53, bottom

Myatt: 57

O'Rourke: 56, top left

Claudia & Bob Osby: 138, 155, 190, 194, 228, 230

Rob Pulleyn: 65

Sontag Rauschke: 53, top

Ralph Schmidt: 56 bottom, 71, 84, 90, 91, 94, 98, 99, 102, 107, 110, 113, 117, 119, 122, 126, 130, 161, 164, 166, 214, 217, 221, 222

David Schoonmaker: 62

Randy Sewell: 54, 55

Fox Watson: 146, 169

## Bird House Painters:

Thom Boswell: 68, 72, 94, 107, 122, 221

Nancy Schoonmaker: 58

Michelle Trafton: 75, 76, 78, 87, 218

Shannon Wood: 71, 84, 90, 91, 98, 99, 102, 110, 113, 117, 119, 126, 130, 222

## Project design assistance by Thom Boswell:

124, 138, 140, 144, 174, 176, 181, 184, 188, 190, 194, 200, 204, 228, 230

Additional Photography by David Schiling: 67

Etchings by Thomas Bewick & his school

## Gallery displays courtesy of:

Blue Spiral I, Asheville, NC: 30, 31, 33, 36, 38, 44, 48

Charles A. Wustum Museum, Racine, WI: 54-56

## Photography location courtesy of:

The Wright Inn, Asheville, NC: 147, 205

## Bird Feed Consultant:

Sally L. Coburn

Every effort has been made to ensure that all information in this book is accurate. However, due to differing conditions, tools, and individual skills, the publisher cannot be responsible for any injuries, losses, or other damages, which may result from the use of the information in this book.

# Artists' Directory

**Ron Anderson**
115 Sue Ann Court
Sterling, VA 22170

**Don Bundrick**
P.O. Box 84
Tallulah Falls, GA 30573

**Carol Costenbader**
34 Deerhaven Lane
Asheville, NC 28803

**Don Daniels**
P.O. Box 939
Locust Grove, OK 74352

**Mark Dockery**
8 Busbee View Road
Asheville, NC 28803

**Mike Durkin**
c/o I. Ellis Johnson School
815 McGirts Bridge Rd.
Laurinburg, NC 28352

**Marshall Fall**
Rt. 1, Box 291-B
Hendersonville, NC 28792

**Debra Fritts**
385 Waverly Hall Circle
Roswell, GA 30075

**Harold Hall**
1203 Lake Martin Drive
Kent, OH 44240

**Bobby Hansson**
P.O. Box 1100
Rising Sun, MD 21911

**Michael Hester**
244-B Swannanoa River Rd.
Asheville, NC 28805

**Mana D.C. Hewitt**
947 Laurie Lane
Columbia, SC 29205

**Bryant Holsenbeck**
2007 Pershing Street
Durham, NC 27705

**Barry Leader**
122 West High Street
Elizabethtown, PA 17022

**Bruce Malicoat**
129 E. Vates Street
Frankenmuth, MI 48734

**Claudia & Bob Osby**
P.O. Box 976
Brevard, NC 28712

**Charles Ratliff**
183 New Avenue
Athens, GA 30601

**David Renfroe**
407 Big Pine Road
Marshall, NC 28753

**Ralph Schmitt**
75 Broadway
Asheville, NC 28801

**Randy Sewell**
38 Muscogee Avenue
Athens, GA 30305

**Susan Starr**
1580 Jones Road
Roswell, GA 30075

**Paul Sumner**
5721 N. Church Street
Greensboro, NC 27405

**Fox Watson**
50 Greene Drive
Black Mountain, NC 28711

**West Olive Folk Art**
8370 160th Avenue
West Olive, MI 49460

# Index

# METRIC EQUIVALENCY

| INCHES | CM |
|--------|------|
| 1/8 | 0.3 |
| 1/4 | 0.6 |
| 3/8 | 1.0 |
| 1/2 | 1.3 |
| 5/8 | 1.6 |
| 3/4 | 1.9 |
| 7/8 | 2.2 |
| 1 | 2.5 |
| 1 1/4 | 3.2 |
| 1 1/2 | 3.8 |
| 1 3/4 | 4.4 |
| 2 | 5.1 |
| 2 1/2 | 6.4 |
| 3 | 7.6 |
| 3 1/2 | 8.9 |
| 4 | 10.2 |
| 4 1/2 | 11.4 |
| 5 | 12.7 |
| 6 | 15.2 |
| 7 | 17.8 |
| 8 | 20.3 |
| 9 | 22.9 |
| 10 | 25.4 |
| 11 | 27.9 |
| 12 | 30.5 |
| 13 | 33.0 |
| 14 | 35.6 |
| 15 | 38.1 |
| 16 | 40.6 |
| 17 | 43.2 |
| 18 | 45.7 |
| 19 | 48.3 |
| 20 | 50.8 |
| 21 | 53.3 |
| 22 | 55.9 |
| 23 | 58.4 |
| 24 | 61.0 |
| 25 | 63.5 |
| 26 | 66.0 |
| 27 | 68.6 |
| 28 | 71.1 |
| 29 | 73.7 |
| 30 | 76.2 |
| 31 | 78.7 |
| 32 | 81.3 |
| 33 | 83.8 |
| 34 | 86.4 |
| 35 | 88.9 |
| 36 | 91.4 |
| 37 | 94.0 |
| 38 | 96.5 |
| 39 | 99.1 |
| 40 | 101.6 |
| 41 | 104.1 |
| 42 | 106.7 |
| 43 | 109.2 |
| 44 | 111.8 |
| 45 | 114.3 |
| 46 | 116.8 |
| 47 | 119.4 |
| 48 | 121.9 |
| 49 | 124.5 |
| 50 | 127.0 |

*Add interest and character to any room with miniature constructions like this schoolhouse (see pages 108-10)*